The New York Times

LARGE-PRINT BRAIN-BOOSTING CROSSWORDS

www.stmartins.com

All of the puzzles that appear in this work were originally published in
The New York Times from February 1, 2012, to June 19, 2012.
Copyright © 2012 by The New York Times Company.
All rights reserved. Reprinted by permission.

ISBN 978-1-250-04925-4

Our books may be purchased in bulk for promotional, educational,
or business use. Please contact your local bookseller or the Macmillan
Corporate and Premium Sales Department at 1-800-221-7945, extension 5442,
or by email at MacmillanSpecialMarkets@macmillan.com.

10   9   8   7

The New York Times

LARGE-PRINT BRAIN-BOOSTING CROSSWORDS
120 Large-Print Puzzles from the Pages of
The New York Times

Edited by Will Shortz

ST. MARTIN'S GRIFFIN ✹ NEW YORK

1 EASY

ACROSS
1. ___ Men ("Who Let the Dogs Out" group)
5. Remove, as pencil marks
10. Ones ranked above cpls.
14. Black, to bards
15. ___ Doone cookies
16. Spanish bull
17. Split a bill evenly with someone
19. Throat clearer
20. Throat dangler
21. "Zip-___-Doo-Dah"
22. Do a fall chore
23. "I've had enough!"
25. Ruble : Russia :: ___ : Poland
27. Milky Way, for one
30. New Zealanders, informally
33. Unrestrained revelry
36. Hot temper
37. Fanglike tooth
38. Prefix with classical
39. Flip out
41. Genetic stuff
42. iPad, for example
44. Flamenco cheer
45. Second to none
46. Old-fashioned music hall
47. Bet on a one-two finish
49. Procrastinator's word
51. Natural barriers between yards
55. Sport that's been called "a good walk spoiled"
57. Pull along
60. Safari animal, informally
61. "___ sow, so shall . . ."
62. Leave the drawers in the drawer, say
64. Speak drunkenly
65. ___-Detoo of "Star Wars"
66. "Understood"
67. Boston ___ (orchestra)
68. Replies to an invitation
69. Former New York mayor Giuliani

DOWN
1. Commenced
2. From the beginning, in Latin
3. Yawn-inducing
4. The clue for 25-Across, e.g.
5. North Pole toymaker
6. Civil rights pioneer Parks
7. Saharan
8. Dwarf who's blessed a lot?
9. Painter's stand
10. Get to work (on)
11. Malfunction
12. Long, hard journey
13. Amount between none and all
18. Dr. Zhivago's love
24. J. Alfred Prufrock's creator T. S. ___
26. "Fine by me"
28. Rainbow's shape
29. Office copy, say
31. Quaint lodgings
32. Plane assignment
33. Not fooled by
34. Librarian's urging
35. Fail financially
37. Prague native
39. Mannerly man, briefly
40. In the style of
43. Casual shoes
45. Kind of day, grooming-wise
47. Blunders
48. Six years, for a U.S. senator
50. Mystery writer's award
52. Infomercial knife
53. Finished
54. "Here, piggy piggy piggy!"
55. [Horrors!]
56. Nobel Peace Prize city
58. When Hamlet dies
59. Sticky stuff
63. Hip-hop's ___ Def

by Tom Pepper

2 EASY

ACROSS

1 "That's lame, dude"
6 ___ Minor
10 Letters starting an address
14 ___ Heep
15 Staffs
16 Indiana's smallest county or the river it touches
17 Imagination, metaphorically
20 Part of a nuclear reactor
21 Zellweger of "Miss Potter"
22 Perform on "Glee," perhaps
23 Featuring top players
25 Gets special attention
27 Sneak a look
28 Investigator of family problems, say
32 Suffix with fool
34 League: Abbr.
35 "Here ___ Again" (1987 #1 hit)
36 Hispaniola's western half
39 Remove the insides from
40 Alternatively
42 Article in Austria
43 Like the food Jack Sprat eats
45 Suffix with confident

46 It's seen in shop windows
49 Opposite of sans
53 Monarchy in the South Pacific
54 Yellowhammer State
56 Very dry, as Champagne
57 Three-masted sailing ship
59 Subtraction game
60 One who's favorably looked upon
63 Fairy tale start
64 Dullea of "2001: A Space Odyssey"
65 Funny Fields
66 Harmonica part
67 Quotes, as a price
68 Observe secretly

DOWN

1 Trumped-up charge
2 Orange-and-black bird
3 Waist reduction aid
4 Nasser's fed.
5 There has been one with every Pixar film since 1998
6 King of gods, in Egyptian myth
7 Burglary target
8 Hobby
9 Pompeii's downfall?
10 More comfy

11 What an easily offended person has
12 High tone?
13 Peas' keeper?
18 Be rude at the dinner table, in a way
19 Its Internet addresses end in .ee
24 Theater playlet
26 Sympathetic syllables
29 Finnish hot spot
30 One of a Freudian trio
31 Balderdash
33 Start of every hour?
36 Up on things, in the '40s
37 Not feel so good
38 Very quickly
39 Andromeda and others
41 Spare tire material
44 Humpty Dumpty, e.g.
45 Marooned, in a way
47 Took the show on the road
48 Duelers' swords
50 Unappealing personal trait . . . or a word that can precede the start of 17-, 28-, 46- or 60-Across
51 Estevez of "The Breakfast Club"
52 City across the Delaware River from Philadelphia

by Mike Buckley

55 Bank nos.
56 Source of ruin
58 Composer
   Satie

60 Supporting
61 Alias letters
62 Move like
   a bunny

3 EASY

ACROSS

1 Yo-Yo Ma's instrument
6 Like most 22-Acrosses
10 Note at the office
14 Disney's "Little Mermaid"
15 Flirty toon Betty ___
16 Persia, today
17 It's kneaded at a bakery
19 PlayStation maker
20 Nine-digit ID
21 Favoritism
22 News and music source
23 "Doonesbury" cartoonist
26 Traveled by inner tube
29 Roman poet who wrote "To be loved, be lovable"
30 German carmaker
31 Port of Yemen
32 401(k) alternative
35 Samuel Beckett play with an unseen character
40 Convent inhabitant
41 Fruit-filled pastry
42 Line of stitches
43 Jacob's brother
44 ___ Palace (Vegas venue)
47 Vito Corleone portrayer
51 Digital publication
52 State north of Calif.
53 Inits. in a military address
56 Speak like Sylvester
57 1954 Hitchcock thriller
60 Dog often messed with by Garfield
61 Wrinkly fruit
62 Wipe chalk from
63 More than want
64 Pie à la ___
65 Japanese noodle soup

DOWN

1 They're often yellow or checkered
2 Makes mistakes
3 Legal claim
4 Meadow
5 Biddy
6 "All ___!" (conductor's cry)
7 Timid
8 Frequent weather condition at the Golden Gate Bridge
9 Speedometer meas.
10 Write 2 + 7 = 10, e.g.
11 Wash away, as a bank
12 Fan frenzy
13 "I'm keeping my eye ___!"
18 Urgent
22 Regretting
23 Trot or canter
24 ___ list
25 Cross-country camper, for short
26 Baby deer
27 Hawaiian feast
28 Chief Norse god
31 Toward the back of a boat
32 Brainstorm
33 Lion's sound
34 $20 bill providers, for short
36 "Don't worry about that"
37 Chicken tikka go-with
38 Vittles
39 ___ buco
43 Ran away to wed
44 Stephen King's first novel
45 Freshly
46 More "out there"
47 Cantaloupe or honeydew
48 Tolerate
49 First name in TV talk
50 Author Dahl
53 Eve's man
54 Sit for a painting
55 Actor Wilson

by Ellen Leuschner and Victor Fleming

57 Bacardi product
58 Psyche part
59 Gun enthusiast's
org.

4 EASY

ACROSS

1 TV shopper's channel
4 Quaint "Oh, don't be silly!"
9 Cathode's counterpart
14 Part of AT&T: Abbr.
15 Period in history
16 Examiner of sunken ships, perhaps
17 Glass of "This American Life"
18 Neighbor of Venice
20 Some makeup
22 RR stop
23 Tweak some text
24 Western Indians
26 Kanye West's genre
28 Cocktails made with Southern Comfort, sloe gin, amaretto and orange juice
36 Anti-bullfighting org.
37 Thing
38 Sign before Virgo
39 With 42-Across, one who might memorize 64-Across?
41 Lower, as the lights
42 See 39-Across
44 Charlottesville sch.
45 "Rats!"
48 Wren den
49 Perfect Sleeper and others
52 Alias
53 Flat bottom?
54 40 acres, maybe
57 N N N, to Greeks
60 Small bus
64 Classical trio found inside 18-, 28- and 49-Across
67 Simple vow
68 What "cheese" produces
69 New Brunswick neighbor
70 Merry
71 Sign of availability
72 Indelicate
73 Medical plan option, for short

DOWN

1 Common makeup applicator
2 Florida's ___ Beach
3 Crab serving
4 Old Spanish coin
5 "I'm tired of your lies"
6 Baby doll
7 Takes steps
8 "Guess ___?"
9 Hubbub
10 School night bedtime, maybe
11 Poet banished by the emperor Augustus
12 Prefix with bel
13 Quod ___ demonstrandum
19 The Marquis de Sade delivered his eulogy
21 United Arab Emirates member
25 Actress Bullock
27 ___ nitrate
28 100
29 Time off
30 Oil from flower petals
31 Time in the service
32 Boundaries
33 "The Lord of the Rings" race
34 Pee Wee of baseball
35 Does some pre-laundry work
40 Fargo's state: Abbr.
43 First stage
46 Big appliance maker
47 Paris and Hector, e.g.
50 "Hot" dish
51 They hold power
54 Partner of hard
55 Cannonballs and such
56 Make muddy
58 "The Few, the Proud . . ." grp.
59 Coal-rich region of Germany
61 Approaching
62 Cheese coated in red wax

by Paula Gamache

63 Fad item of 1962
65 Bumped into
66 Hamm of
soccer

5 EASY

ACROSS

1 Patriot Allen with the Green Mountain Boys
6 Things "bursting in air"
11 With 17-Across, value of some opinions
14 Pageant headgear
15 Sans-serif typeface
16 Many, many years
17 See 11-Across
18 *Some reddish-orange caviar
20 Work unit
21 Silent performer
22 Renders null
23 *Major road
27 Steve of "The Office"
28 Prisoner
31 *Nancy Pelosi was the first person ever to have this title in Congress
35 Hypothetical cases
38 French king
39 Driver's licenses and such, in brief
40 *Parliamentary procedure
47 Big supermarket chain
48 See 26-Down
52 February occasion, some of whose honorees can be found in the answers to the five starred clues
56 Four straight wins to start the World Series, e.g.
58 Tidy
59 Ash holder
60 *Really hunger for
62 Had title to
64 Buckeyes' sch.
65 Snoozed
66 World, in Italian
67 Mind-reading skill, for short
68 Part of the body above the waist
69 Show of overwhelming love

DOWN

1 "And so on, and so on"
2 ___ del Fuego
3 Where airplanes are repaired
4 "A work of ___ is a confession": Camus
5 "If I Ruled the World" rapper
6 Fundamental
7 Commercial suffix akin to "à go-go"
8 Distance runner
9 Blast sound
10 Ljubljana dweller
11 Dish marinated in sweetened soy sauce
12 Lumber
13 Low bills
19 "___ Rae" (Sally Field film)
21 Not very spicy
24 Not masc.
25 State south of Ga.
26 With 48-Across, leader of the House of Representatives, 1977–87
29 Turner who founded CNN
30 Hesitant sounds
32 Dog sound
33 Cow sound
34 Francis Drake, Isaac Newton or Mix-a-Lot
35 Needle
36 PETA target
37 What a ramp does
41 White-feathered wader
42 Purposely ignore
43 Surgery sites, for short
44 Word before know and care
45 Suffix with differ
46 Hi-___ monitor
49 "No idea"
50 Texas city on the Rio Grande

by Samuel A. Donaldson

51 The "L" of L.B.J.
53 Bury
54 Areas explored by submarines

55 Keep one's ___ the ground
56 ___ gin fizz
57 Scaredy-cat

61 ___-Jo ('88 Olympics track star)
62 Meditation sounds
63 "Holy moly!"

6 EASY

ACROSS

1 "OMG ur so funny!"
4 "You flatter me too much!"
10 Vatican locale
14 "Who ___?"
15 Complain
16 Any of the singers of the 1973 #1 hit "Love Train"
17 Something to hang your hat on
18 "Platoon" director
20 "That tastes awful!" comments
22 Leandro's partner in a Handel title
23 Camel refueling spots
24 Comedian who voiced the lead role in "Ratatouille"
28 It gets flatter as it gets older
29 Little blobs on slides
33 Material for a military uniform
35 Vassal
37 Peculiar
38 Tom Cruise's "Risky Business" co-star
42 Fury
43 Mtn. stats
44 Sonnets and such
45 Big cake maker
48 Paneled rooms, often

49 Igor player in "Young Frankenstein"
54 Audibly amazed
57 Old nuclear regulatory org.
58 Modern prefix with mom
59 What the starts of 18-, 24-, 38- and 49-Across each won
63 Navy noncom
64 "Fifteen Miles on the ___ Canal"
65 Necessary
66 Symbol of sturdiness
67 Blue-green shade
68 Sends to the dump
69 Soph., jr. and sr.

DOWN

1 Drink greedily
2 Ω
3 "Star Wars" weapon
4 Gold, in Guadalupe
5 State capital whose main street is named Last Chance Gulch
6 Vice president Agnew
7 Saves for later viewing, in a way
8 2000 Beatles album or its peak chart position
9 The "p" of r.p.m.
10 Spin on an axis

11 13-Down, south of the border
12 Neck line?
13 11-Down, north of the border
19 Unaided
21 Feed, as a fire
25 Like much of Pindar's work
26 They might be hawked
27 Kind of radio
30 Sci-fi physician played by DeForest Kelley
31 Leading man?
32 Ben & Jerry's competitor
33 ___ Kross ('90s rap duo)
34 Juno, in Greece
35 Bob of "How I Met Your Mother"
36 N.Y.C. summer hrs.
39 "If I Could Turn Back Time" singer, 1989
40 German car
41 Sonata part
46 Brew named for a Dutch river
47 Nordic native
48 Edict
50 Rowdy ___, "Rawhide" cowboy
51 Fights that go on and on
52 For face value
53 Crannies

by Caleb Madison

54 Help in crime
55 Actor Richard
56 Most of Turkey
is in it

60 Stat that a QB doesn't
want to be high: Abbr.
61 Corp. honcho
62 Mag. staff

ACROSS

1 ___ Longstocking (children's story character)
6 Dating from
10 Shaping tool
14 Energy giant that filed for bankruptcy in 2001
15 Rob of "Parks and Recreation"
16 Relative of a frog
17 Exhibits pride
19 Hens lay them
20 Calc prerequisite
21 Fine and dandy
22 "Loud and clear, bro"
24 ___ Vegas
25 Betray a lover's confidences
29 Lashes grow from it
31 Confederate general at Gettysburg
32 ___ v. Wade
33 Surround with a saintly light
36 Craps table surface
37 Symbol of embezzlement
41 Landlord's due
42 Surface for an unpaved road
43 Docs' grp.
44 Abbr. on a garment sale tag
46 2001 Sean Penn movie
50 E-ZPass pays it
54 Israeli gun
55 One of nine on a Clue board
56 Water, when it gets cold enough
57 Greek H's
58 Spirited horse
60 Group with the 1971 3× platinum album "Aqualung"
63 Bough
64 Vogue rival
65 "Gay" city
66 Small bouquet
67 Wedding cake feature
68 Place

DOWN

1 Mortar's partner
2 Place for arriving office papers
3 Kudos
4 Ping-___
5 Neither Rep. nor Dem.
6 Voices above tenors
7 Good long baths
8 Avian hooter
9 Catlike
10 Suffered ignominious failure, in slang
11 High-class poetry it isn't
12 Zig's opposite
13 Workers with mss.
18 Greeted informally
23 Ike's inits.
25 Ilk
26 Honolulu hello
27 Laze
28 Court do-over
30 Gave temporarily
34 Wrathful
35 8½" × 11" paper size: Abbr.
36 "Annie" or "Annie Hall"
37 Prefix with sphere
38 "Slot machines" and "cash lost in 'em," e.g.
39 More fiendish
40 Freshwater duck
41 "Go team!"
44 ___ Jima
45 Kind of engine for an airplane
47 Sew up, as a wound
48 Rhododendron relative
49 Deceived
51 Model building or stamp collecting
52 "Annie" or "Annie Hall"
53 Autumn hue
57 Coup d'___

by Bill Thompson

58 Swiss peak
59 ___ de Janeiro
61 QB Manning
62 Photo ___

ACROSS

1 Norwegian city
5 Corrida shouts
9 Start of a carol
14 Proceed slowly
15 Explorer Marco
16 Mississippi, e.g.
17 "Othello"
bad guy
18 Port of Algeria
19 Modern Persian
20 Hint—first part
23 KLM competitor
24 Pres. Obama,
once
25 Public hanging?
28 Magical dragon
31 Words of relief
36 Café lightener
38 Less's opposite
40 Seating choice
41 Hint's next part
44 Buddy List user
45 Father of a foal
46 Bumper blemish
47 Derisive looks
49 Bugler's melody
51 Hogs' enclosure
52 Surreal ending?
54 Tiny brain size
56 Last of the hint
65 Half a wolf's cry
66 Daily delivery
67 Odd collection
68 From square one
69 Old Dodge
model

70 Lacking starch
71 Most egregious
72 Caught sight of
73 Glasgow lovely

DOWN

1 Boy of Mayberry
2 Serbian or Pole
3 Box in a theater
4 Secret targets?
5 Pogo and others
6 Actress Singer
7 Personal flair
8 Vocalizations
9 Eastern, in a way
10 Mag.'s statistic
11 Nascar circuit
12 List on a laptop
13 Sandusky's lake
21 Incessant talk
22 Grazing ground
25 False identity
26 Blathered away
27 Duke or duchess
29 Beau Brummells
30 Mango and guava
32 Wasn't truthful
33 Hearth residue
34 Not be vertical
35 Short-tempered
37 You, in the Bible
39 Pound of poetry
42 Pain in the neck
43 Former airship
48 Opposite of NNW
50 Filming locale
53 Internal notes

55 Coral reef isle
56 Melting period
57 Boss of fashion
58 Beam in a bridge
59 Baseball stats
60 Facebook entry
61 Bit of dialogue
62 Director Kazan
63 Canyon locales
64 Absorbs, with "up"

by Randall J. Hartman

ACROSS

1 Nickname for Louis Armstrong
6 Plain as day
11 Apply with a cotton ball, say
14 Table of data, e.g.
15 Challenger
16 School's URL ending
17 Hirsute carnival attraction
19 Writer Anaïs
20 Order of coffee in a small cup
21 Roved
23 Pink
24 Trying to make sense of
26 Apollo 11's destination
28 Stave off, as a disaster
29 Arouse from sleep
32 Computer file extension
33 "Hmm, I guess so"
36 ___-Wan Kenobi
37 Hit HBO series set in Baltimore
41 "Evil Woman" rock grp.
42 Clark ___, Superman's alter ego
44 Lumberjack's tool
45 Gridiron units

47 Dwarves' representative in the Fellowship of the Ring
49 Skeptic's rejoinder
51 Eleventh hour
54 Rick's love in "Casablanca"
58 Cause of "I" strain?
59 Inquisition targets
61 Chest bone
62 Children's game hinted at by the circled letters
64 TiVo, for one, in brief
65 Inventor Howe
66 Hit the accelerator
67 Mediterranean, e.g.
68 Hear again, as a case
69 Simple kind of question

DOWN

1 Cavalry sword
2 "You ___ stupid!"
3 Pitfalls
4 Request from a tired child
5 Jekyll's alter ego
6 Most likely to win, as a favorite
7 Bravery
8 ___ of Good Feelings
9 1948 John Wayne western

10 Sign on a tray of samples
11 Scouting mission leader?
12 "Goodbye, mon ami!"
13 Kind of cake that's ring-shaped
18 Gas brand with a tiger symbol
22 Farming: Prefix
25 Cab
27 Province west of Que.
29 Chinese cooker
30 Lincoln, informally
31 World's longest venomous snake
32 Rams fan?
34 Obsolete
35 Some boxing wins, for short
38 One-third the length of the Belmont Stakes
39 Interstate sign with an arrow
40 Ogle
43 ___ torch (outdoor party lighting)
46 Up for discussion
48 One in a pit at a concert
49 "Whatever you want"
50 Capital of Switzerland
51 "Study, study, study" types

by Mike Nothnagel

52 "Just tell me the answer"
53 Start of a rumor
55 Property claims
56 Welcome at the front door
57 Invite out for
60 A little "out there," as humor
63 Dah's counterpart in Morse code

ACROSS
1 Salon offering
5 America's 44th
10 Current units
14 ___ Rios, Jamaica
15 Currently airing
16 Look sullen
17 "So what?!"
20 Schedule
21 ___ From Hawaii (1973 Elvis concert)
22 Kind of store
23 Elizabethan ___
25 Beginnings of embryos
27 "So what?!"
36 Surgeons' workplaces, for short
37 Beginning
38 Pago Pago's place
39 Number two son
41 Stockpile
43 Israel's first king
44 Bridgestones, e.g.
46 Condos, e.g.
48 British verb ending
49 "So what?!"
52 Viewed
53 Site of the smallest bone in the body
54 Hot tub locale
57 The fellas in "GoodFellas"
61 Slender game fishes
65 "So what?!"
68 As well
69 One who has no chance
70 "The Time Machine" leisure class
71 Savvies
72 Puts in the hold
73 Transmitted

DOWN
1 Pea protectors
2 Environmental sci.
3 ___ Silvia, mother of Romulus and Remus
4 "Fiddler on the Roof" star
5 Toronto's prov.
6 ___ Raton, Fla.
7 M.P.'s target
8 Like early Elvis albums
9 Diane Sawyer, for one
10 Mar. follower
11 "___ Lisa"
12 Shell fixture
13 Dance move
18 Propeller-heads
19 Icicle sites
24 Ones putting out feelers
26 "Regrettably . . ."
27 Raccoon relative
28 Go round and round
29 Rehab seekers
30 Actress O'Neal
31 Old pal
32 "___ to the Moon" (seminal 1902 sci-fi film)
33 Cybermessage
34 Boozehound
35 House of the Seven Gables locale
40 Camera part
42 To be, in Tours
45 "Me, too"
47 Like a bubble bath
50 Regional accents
51 Unethical payoffs
54 Impediment
55 Copernicus, e.g., by birth
56 Helper: Abbr.
58 Pick up, as a bill
59 Kelly Clarkson's "___ One Will Listen"
60 Several
62 Moolah
63 Subj. for a Fed chairman
64 Short comic sketch
66 Mike Tyson stat
67 Miss, after vows

by Wesley Johnson

ACROSS

1 German cry
4 Ice-grabbing tool
9 Bid
14 Genetic stuff
15 Cutting one may bring tears to your eyes
16 Mrs. Gorbachev
17 Oct. follower
18 Had a big influence on Philip's music?
20 Bothered terribly
22 Envision
23 "Enough already!"
24 Fanatics
27 Grey who wrote about the Old West
29 Harshly criticized Danielle's novels?
34 ___ Guevara
36 Starch from a tropical palm
37 Company that created Pong
38 The "L" in S&L
40 ___ decongestant
43 Norway's capital
44 Chef's wear
46 Clickable computer image
48 Hankering
49 Scared the daylights out of Elijah in "The Lord of the Rings"?
53 Soft powder
54 Bleepers
57 ___ as it is
60 British ref. for wordsmiths
62 Deplete
63 Trounced Chris in a comedy competition?
67 NBC comedy show since '75
68 Be in harmony
69 Lacking justification
70 Rightmost number on a grandfather clock
71 Veg out
72 Keats and Shelley
73 Charge for a bang-up job?

DOWN

1 Desi of "I Love Lucy"
2 100 smackers
3 "Show some mercy!"
4 Native American drums
5 Yoko from Tokyo
6 Zero
7 "Ye ___!"
8 Eruption that might elicit a blessing
9 Web site alternative to com or edu
10 Unnaturally high voice
11 Italian carmaker
12 Canadian gas brand
13 Speak with a gravelly voice
19 Utterly exhausted
21 State between Miss. and Ga.
25 I.R.S. agent, e.g., informally
26 Company whose mascot is Sonic the Hedgehog
28 Org. protecting U.S. secrets
30 Symbolic riveter of W.W. II
31 "Careful!"
32 Mystery writer ___ Stanley Gardner
33 Leo's symbol
34 Applaud
35 Optimist's feeling
39 Watery expanse between England and Scandinavia
41 High-voltage Australian band?
42 Actor Rob of "The West Wing"
45 Vardalos of "My Big Fat Greek Wedding"
47 Peacenik's mantra
50 Floating arctic mass
51 Became a winter hazard, as a road
52 W.W. II intelligence org.

by Lynn Lempel

55 Quarrel
56 Bowler's challenge
57 Battle reminder
58 Goad
59 Ringlet
61 James Bond's film debut
64 Evil spell
65 Keats or Shelley work
66 Abridge

ACROSS
1 Above
5 Badly rough up
9 Despot's desire
14 Wife whose face was never seen on "Cheers"
15 Art Deco artist
16 Response to "Am not!"
17 Awestruck
18 Tons
19 Group valuing high I.Q.'s
20 *"Everyone off!"
22 *Exactly right
23 NATO part: Abbr.
24 Put-it-together-yourself company
26 Toon Mr. ___
28 *Often-restricted zone
33 Thanksgiving side dish
34 Cow catcher
36 Loft's locale
37 *Bag remover, of a sort
39 *Jumper alternative
42 Singers of "Voulez-Vous" and "Waterloo"
43 Heroic Schindler
45 Many a "Star Trek" officer: Abbr.
46 *Wrestling move
49 Good to go
51 Norse prankster
52 Limit

53 *Deckhand, e.g.
57 Unfruitful paths . . . or a description of both words in the answers to the seven starred clues?
62 "In the raw," "in the red" or "in the running"
63 Architect with an avian name
64 Cancel
65 Assassin in black
66 When repeated, a Polynesian island
67 Heroine in one of Salinger's "Nine Stories"
68 Four Holy Roman emperors
69 U.S.M.C. truant
70 "Man and Superman" playwright

DOWN
1 Ellipsoidal
2 Singer Suzanne
3 Cupid's Greek counterpart
4 Shabby
5 Beefy entree
6 Janis's partner in the funnies
7 Shangri-las
8 Court cry
9 Patagonian plains

10 Snack with a Double Stuf variety
11 Departed
12 Gas brand with a tiger symbol
13 Horse hue
21 Popular vodka, informally
22 Sun. message
25 Mall info source
26 Evasive response
27 Tiny creature
29 "Masterpiece Theatre" network
30 Reacted to a massage, maybe
31 Old pal
32 "The Lord of the Rings" tree creatures
33 "Woo-hoo!"
35 Keep on the shelves
38 Boy
40 What an otoscope explores
41 Tire feature
44 Hobos' hangout
47 Alpaca cousins
48 Suffix with ball
50 High points
53 ___-Soviet relations
54 Move text around
55 Isn't incorrect?
56 "Mr. ___ Risin'" (Jim Morrison biography)
58 Architect Saarinen

by Jeff Chen

59 Snack
60 Russian legislature
61 Beefy entree
63 Ring org.

13 EASY

ACROSS

1 From Athens, say
6 Sharp product from Sharp
10 Labyrinth
14 "___ Vice"
15 Days long past
16 ___ contraceptive
17 Image on an Indian pole
18 Destitute
19 Redding who sang "The Dock of the Bay"
20 Academy Award winner for playing 46-Across
23 Backbone
25 Let out, as a fishing line
26 Academy Award winner for playing 46-Across
30 "Can't Get It Out of My Head" rock grp.
31 Clear part of blood
32 Either the first or last vowel sound in "Alaska"
36 Stratford-upon-___
38 Africa's northernmost capital
40 Actress Madeline of "Blazing Saddles"
41 Lite
43 Guadalajara girls
45 Pedantic quibble
46 Academy Award-winning role for both 20- and 26-Across
49 Vie (for)
52 Eagle's home
53 Academy Award-winning film released in March 1972
57 ___ Major (constellation)
58 Actress Skye of "Say Anything . . ."
59 Place for gold to be stored
63 Encounter
64 Large coffee holders
65 Follow
66 Rose of the diamond
67 Butcher's stock
68 Wild West transport

DOWN

1 World clock std.
2 ___ de Janeiro
3 Consume
4 Lagasse in the kitchen
5 Japanese robes
6 Ballyhoo
7 "Let's Make a Deal" choice
8 Gait not as fast as a canter
9 W.W. I's longest battle
10 Object retrieved on an Apollo mission
11 Clarinetist Shaw
12 Congo, from 1971 to 1997
13 Spanish-language newspaper that brings "light" to its readers
21 Author Stephen Vincent ___
22 Termini
23 Blast from the side of a warship
24 Homework problem in geometry
26 Brunch or dinner
27 Sacha Baron Cohen alter ego
28 Ancient kind of alphabet
29 Protein-building acid
33 Vietnam's capital
34 Complain annoyingly
35 Initial stake
37 Steer
39 Politico Palin
42 What may give pause to couch potatoes?
44 What tank tops lack
47 Ho-humness
48 Straying
49 Tree remnant
50 Number of little pigs or blind mice

by Jeremy Horwitz

51 Put back to zero, say
54 Golfer's cry
55 "___ and the King of Siam"
56 Examination
60 Anytown, ___
61 Schlep
62 Links peg

ACROSS

1 Ado
7 Queen in a speech by Mercutio
10 Denizen of the Endor world in "Return of the Jedi"
14 Two-thirds of AOL
15 Hole in one
16 "___ le roi!"
17 Danish birthplace of Hans Christian Andersen
18 Not that many
20 One who engages in finger painting
22 TV announcer Hall
23 "That's it!"
24 Broadcasts
25 Ados
27 Give a makeover
31 "Take a Chance on Me" group
34 Detective's aid
36 Mount ___ Hospital
37 One who engages in fingerprinting
40 Promotional device
41 When said three times, 1970 film on the Pearl Harbor attack
42 Whip
43 Target as a customer
45 What "bis" means
47 Tug hard
49 Unwell
50 Prefix with bar
53 One who engages in finger-pointing
57 Ecstatic
58 Van Gogh painting dominated by green and blue
59 Starting from
60 Soapmaker's supply
61 Title of hits by Elvis Presley and Justin Bieber
62 Roller coaster cry
63 On the ___ (fleeing)
64 Locale in Devon or New Hampshire

DOWN

1 Pioneering scientist Robert
2 Reversed
3 Mixture
4 Tricky situation
5 Open, as an envelope
6 Locale of a 1923 Munich putsch
7 Goya subject
8 Lexus rival
9 Rouse
10 Indiana city on the Ohio
11 Ring bearer
12 No longer in love with
13 ___ Gardens
19 Nobel winner Mother ___
21 Observe with the mouth open
25 Standard sitcom subject
26 Wooden shoe
28 Novelist Seton
29 Part of W.M.D.
30 Heart of the matter
31 Book after John
32 Creamy cheese
33 Jessica of "The Illusionist"
35 Traveler on the Beagle
38 Involve
39 Salon tool
44 Available if needed
46 Bleach brand
48 Home of Barack Obama Sr.
50 "No more for me"
51 Terse note from the boss
52 Canadian figure skating champion Brian
53 Exhortation during labor
54 Cousin of a bassoon
55 Agenda part
56 Split
57 Tyrannosaurus rex had a big one

by Will Nediger

15 EASY

ACROSS

1 Antlered animal
4 Provided with meals
7 With 58-Down, vehicle for people on the go? . . . or a hint to five strategically placed answers in this puzzle
13 Alternative to chocolate
15 Musical performance
16 Low-cost, as an airplane seat
17 1920s–30s design style
18 Time of change
19 Intl. feminine group
20 Feminine title
21 Sir Walter Scott novel
23 Bouquet holders
25 Spy's knowledge, informally
27 Singer/actress Deanna of the 1930s–40s
29 Pinocchio, at times
30 "___ about time!"
31 Complained loudly
35 90° angle
36 Native of Cuba's capital
38 Cry for a matador
39 Rarely

41 Charged particle
42 ___ Nostra
43 Square dance maneuver
45 Senegal's capital
46 Was wide open
49 State of bliss
51 King Kong, for one
52 The second of the five W's
54 Roma is its capital
57 From one of the Baltics
59 Suffered an embarrassing defeat
60 Group artistically, as flowers
61 Desert procession
62 Smells to high heaven
63 Chicago trains
64 Brian of ambient music

DOWN

1 Not odd
2 Fabric that doesn't block much light
3 Smart aleck, say
4 Bouquet-related
5 Violinist Mischa
6 24 hours
7 Bygone Ford car, informally
8 General who became the first emperor of Rome

9 YouTube posting, for short
10 10 ___ or less (supermarket checkout sign)
11 Mother-of-pearl
12 Lip ___
14 Words often declared after "Well"
15 Colder and wetter, as weather
19 "Absolutely right!"
22 RCA or Samsung product
24 "Wheel of Fortune" purchase
25 Parts of a French archipelago
26 Cleopatra's river
28 Kellogg's All-___
30 Big name in pet food
32 "Don't just stand there!"
33 Lohengrin's love
34 Beloved
36 Snooker
37 Jordan's Queen ___
40 J.F.K.'s predecessor
42 Where Hudson Bay is
44 Nonsensical
45 Some office stamps
46 Fancy affairs
47 Separately
48 ___ dish (lab holder)
50 Life-sustaining
53 Long-haired uglies

by Ray Fontenot

55 Persia, now
56 Zinc's is 30: Abbr.
58 See 7-Across
59 One-spot card

ACROSS

1 Insignificant one
6 One in a black suit
11 Tie-breaking voters in the Sen.
14 Not as mad
15 Gave support
16 Talent agent Emanuel
17 Investigative reporter's specialty
20 Smoke column
21 Einstein's birthplace
22 Used a loom
23 Group within a group
25 Fenway Park team, familiarly
26 Half-___ (coffee order)
29 ___ Lanka
30 Lead-in to preservation
32 City where "Peer Gynt" premiered
34 Previously
36 Disc-shaped vacuum cleaner from iRobot
40 Bit of pirate booty
43 "Naughty!"
44 Have dinner
45 Depressed
46 Jalopy
48 Poker legend Ungar
50 ___ Poke (candy brand)
51 New person on the job
54 Badly bothering
57 La Salle of "ER"
58 Separator of syllables in many dictionaries
59 It takes a bow in an orchestra
62 Gather wealth by exploitation . . . as hinted at by this puzzle's shaded squares?
66 It may be used with a plunger
67 Declaration of Independence signer?
68 Online memo
69 Nay's opposite
70 Overused
71 Antianxiety medication

DOWN

1 Measure for a batter?: Abbr.
2 Measure of speed in "Star Trek"
3 Hydroxyl compound
4 Puzzle with its pluses and minuses?
5 First, in Latin
6 Lack muscle tone, perhaps
7 Tick off
8 They're not kids anymore
9 View to be
10 Newsroom workers, for short
11 Sony laptops
12 Home of Brigham Young University
13 Vicks decongestant brand
18 The Cornhuskers
19 Double
24 Weary reaction
25 Lava lamp formation
26 Were priced at
27 Saharan slitherers
28 Criticism
31 Prone to violence
33 Privately
35 "___ bodkins!"
37 "Old MacDonald Had a Farm" sounds
38 Many a New Year's Day game
39 Word usually abbreviated on timelines
41 "No need to elaborate"
42 Kick out
47 Midwest city representing average tastes
49 Like some hair salons
51 Sizable
52 Woman's name meaning "peace"
53 Wild West show prop
55 Coral Sea sight
56 "We're Not ___ Take It" ("Tommy" tune)
58 Numbers follower: Abbr.

by Todd McClary

60 Defense secretary Panetta

61 "The Thin Man" canine

63 Command posts, for short

64 N.Y. Mets' div.

65 Cowhand handle

17 EASY

ACROSS

1 In different places
6 Girls with coming-out parties
10 Bro's counterpart
13 Meddles
14 Jai ___
15 Walk with a hitch
16 Relaxing spot on a veranda
18 World's fair, e.g.
19 Band of secret agents
20 Make a difference
22 Web site ID
23 Huge success at the box office
25 Braid
28 Twosome
29 Cribbage marker
30 Fluffy stuff caught in the dryer
31 Tiny hollow cylinder
33 Stick up
36 Late singer Winehouse
37 Virginia site of two Civil War battles
38 Attorneys' org.
39 N.B.A.'s 7'6" ___ Ming
40 Eyeing amorously
41 Person on a pedestal
42 Set down
44 Ambulance letters
45 Prepare to propose, perhaps
46 Hillside threat after a heavy rain
49 Prefix with day or night
50 Song that people stand to sing
51 Lopsided victory
55 Tennis's Nastase
56 Sheet music for Van Cliburn, say
59 Makes less bright
60 Title for Byron or Baltimore
61 A– and C+
62 Sault ___ Marie
63 Laughs over some unsophisticated humor
64 German Surrealist Max

DOWN

1 Downloads for tablets
2 Stagehand's responsibility
3 Well-ventilated
4 Army enlistee
5 Jeans topper
6 Deputy ___ (toon)
7 Manning who has won multiple Super Bowl M.V.P. awards
8 Prohibit
9 Greek "S"
10 Traditional start of middle school
11 Architect for the Louvre pyramid
12 Athlete's pursuit
15 River through Hades
17 Irreverent weekend show, briefly
21 Colorado ski town
23 Glorious
24 Grieves for
25 With 35-Down, much-anticipated cry every April
26 Peru's capital
27 "Whenever you feel like it"
28 Made less sharp
31 Yank
32 Schlep
34 Bassoon relative
35 See 25-Down
37 2009 British singing sensation Susan
41 Big series name in auto racing
43 Smokers' residue
45 Instruction to Kate in a Cole Porter musical
46 Eight milkers in "The 12 Days of Christmas"
47 Pitch-dark
48 Suggest
49 China's Long March leader
51 Extremities

by Lynn Lempel

52 Showing signs of use
53 Annoys
54 It might be out
on a limb

57 Acknowledgment
of debt, in brief
58 State north
of La.

ACROSS

1 Morning times, for short
4 Come to pass
9 Chose, with "for"
14 Vital fluid
15 Hangman's halter
16 Bones below the tibia
17 Top prize in the Juegos Olímpicos
18 Mosquito Magnets and flypaper
20 Snack chips made from corn
22 Loving to bits
23 Campers' lightweight cover-ups
26 Opposite of old, in Germany
27 Gathering clouds, e.g.
28 Amo, ___, amat
29 Whistles of relief
31 Hump day: Abbr.
32 Winter forecast
33 Sermon server
34 Eater of lean, in rhyme
36 Like the bathroom after a hot shower
39 Restaurant chain with syrup dispensers on every table
40 Gymgoer's pride
43 Tough guys
44 Narrow cut
45 One of several on a French door
46 Always, in sonnets
47 Feature of a gladiator sandal
49 How some professional services are offered
52 Modern sight on many an Indian reservation
53 Working components of an engine . . . or what the ends of 18-, 23-, 34- and 47-Across are?
56 '60s teach-in grp.
57 Missouri river to the Missouri River
58 Spirit of a culture
59 French pronoun
60 Gives a darn?
61 "Likely ___!"
62 Six-foot runner?

DOWN

1 At present
2 Words from an aspiring fiancé
3 Bratty, say
4 Source of the headline "World Death Rate Holding Steady at 100 Percent," with "The"
5 Faithfulness
6 S&P 500 listings: Abbr.
7 Put into service
8 Quick summaries
9 ___ von Bismarck
10 Catherine who was the last wife of Henry VIII
11 Instructor's charge
12 Disney-owned cable broadcaster of game highlights
13 Gross out
19 Causes of end zone celebrations, for short
21 Big weight
24 Wildly
25 Nubby fabric derived from a cocoon
29 Shawl or stole
30 Batter's datum
32 ___ Club (Costco competitor)
33 Knight, to a damsel
34 Binge
35 Punxsutawney ___ (Groundhog Day celeb)
36 Second wife, to the hubby's kids
37 Bette Midler film loosely based on Janis Joplin's life
38 Old Volkswagen seven-seater
40 Coffeehouse server
41 Endlessly
42 Withdrawal's opposite
44 ___.com (urban myth debunker)

by Paula Gamache

45 Components of
   scores: Abbr.
47 Film director
   Lee
48 Fresh, in an
   impolite way
50 Home of the
   Cowboys, informally
51 Individuals
54 Lawyer:
   Abbr.
55 Fraternity "P"

ACROSS

1 Wine barrel
5 Tear to pieces
10 "Porgy and ___"
14 Words after "here," "there" and "everywhere" in "Old MacDonald Had a Farm"
15 "Pet" annoyance
16 For grades 1–12
17 Negative reaction to failure
19 Emergency-related
20 Snake along the Nile
21 Dublin's land
22 Former congresswoman Bella
23 Sort of words that sailors are famous for
27 Flip over
29 Synthesizer designer Robert
30 Circumvent
31 It's about six feet for a turkey vulture
35 ___ de Janeiro
36 Other half of a hit 45
38 Refinery material
39 Source of the word "karma"
42 Ken and Barbie
44 Deadly 1966 hurricane with a Spanish-derived name
45 "Cats" poet
47 Feuding families, e.g.
51 Chilling, as Champagne
52 Purple spring bloomer
53 Drunk's interjection
56 Fascinated by
57 Sugar craving
60 Sewing line
61 Like names starting "Ff-"
62 Unadulterated
63 Sea eagles
64 English class assignment
65 River of Hades

DOWN

1 Spanish house
2 "Famous" cookie man
3 Chowder eater's utensil
4 Seoul's home: Abbr.
5 Perfume application
6 When repeated, a crier's cry
7 Ward off
8 Preceding night
9 ___ Moines Register
10 Mattress invaders
11 "My Fair Lady" lady
12 Shoulder gesture
13 Long, drawn-out attack
18 Icy cold
22 Awestruck
24 "___ live and breathe!"
25 Surrounded by
26 All's opposite
27 Autos
28 Athletic shoe brand
31 A lively person may have a sparkling one
32 Remove, as scratches on an auto
33 Singer Guthrie
34 Egg holder
36 ___ Rabbit
37 Evaluate, with "up"
40 "2 Broke Girls" and "30 Rock"
41 Place for a football pad
42 Certain believer
43 Corrida cheer
45 Mother ___ of Calcutta
46 Horseshoe forger
47 Capital of Idaho
48 ___ circle
49 Largest moon of Saturn
50 Quantum mechanics pioneer Bohr
54 Modest response to praise
55 Follower of Corn, Rice and Wheat in cereal names
57 Neighbor of Nor.
58 Craven of horror films
59 Photo ___ (political events)

by Nancy Kavanaugh

20 EASY

ACROSS
1. Beams
5. "Nuts!"
10. Had more than a feeling
14. Region
15. Central Florida city
16. Singer with a reputation for being self-centered
17. Site for a diet of worms?
18. Wheeling, Cincinnati and Louisville are in it
20. Longtime Nicaraguan president
22. Smoked herring
23. Hollywood's Henry, Jane or Peter
26. Instrument that's played by turning a crank
29. Shaq's game
32. Old Italian coin
33. Trio after Q
35. Shoreline flier
36. Adorn with jewels
38. It's not butter
39. Truck scale unit
40. 1970s Chevy
41. Track shapes
42. Citrus fruit originally grown in Brazil
46. Director Eastwood
47. Eat away at

51. Plot device used in "Freaky Friday" . . . or a hint to the interior of 20-, 26- or 42-Across
54. Womanish
57. ___ breve (2/2 time)
58. Drug unit
59. Bruce of "Sherlock Holmes" films
60. What a milkmaid holds
61. God with a bow and arrow
62. Utopias
63. Creepy-sounding lake name?

DOWN
1. Genre for Smokey Robinson
2. "That's ___ shame"
3. Kind of question
4. Like an appetite that can be fulfilled
5. Car ___
6. Late NPR newsman
7. "Aquarius" musical
8. Very much
9. Repeating shape on an oscilloscope
10. "Constant Craving" singer
11. Zilch
12. New Year's ___
13. Route
19. Lead-in to phobia

21. List ender
24. Alfalfa's girl in "The Little Rascals"
25. Photographer Adams
27. "Pomp and Circumstance" composer
28. Golfer's concern
29. "Wanna ___?"
30. Rodeo bucker
31. One for the record books?
34. How-___
36. Railway encircling a city
37. It may be inflated
38. Think too highly of
40. Poison
41. Purple people eater, e.g.
43. Red-eyed birds
44. Winning blackjack combo
45. Dickens's output
48. Physician Sir William
49. ___ Lama
50. Thrill
52. Oklahoma city
53. Fury
54. Barely make, with "out"
55. It's green year-round
56. "Alice" waitress

by Gregory Philip Butler

ACROSS

1 Yankee's crosstown rival
4 Burro
7 Aunts' little girls
13 Lion's locks
14 ___ constrictor
15 "So fancy!"
16 Assns.
17 Sexy sort
19 Playing marble
21 Grp. that raids grow houses
22 Cry of surprise
23 Influential sort
28 Compass pointer
29 Bread eaten during Passover
33 Photocopier malfunctions
34 Israeli carrier
37 Tired
38 Cry to a matador
39 Amiable sort
41 Tree juice
42 Gandhi, e.g., religiously
44 "Gladiator" garment
45 Yearn (for)
46 Word after "force of" or "freak of"
48 Encouragement
50 Supple sort
54 Cigar residue
57 Opposite of post-
58 Rather distrustful
59 Precious sort
64 New York theater award
65 Place for pizza or ice cream
66 Put two and two together, say
67 Caterer's coffee containers
68 Feature on a skunk's back
69 Parcel of property
70 Feeling blue

DOWN

1 Reader's notes alongside the text
2 Usual wedding precursor
3 Exam takers
4 Stomach muscles, for short
5 Drunkard
6 Riyadh native
7 Polite refusal to a lady
8 Debtor's letters
9 Worker in Santa's workshop
10 Bistro
11 Nobelist Wiesel
12 Plummeted
13 Biblical kingdom east of the Dead Sea
18 Dover's state: Abbr.
20 Finish
24 Royal role for Liz Taylor
25 Serf
26 Cartoondom's Deputy ___
27 Chowed down
30 Spelling clarification that Aziz might use twice
31 Common marmalade ingredient
32 Ballyhoo
33 Adams, Tyler or Kennedy
35 Hullabaloo
36 Advantage
39 Spiritual teacher of a 42-Across
40 Teri of "Tootsie"
43 "That's obvious, stupid!"
45 Pathetic
47 Order of the British ___
49 Hairspray alternative
51 "Diamonds ___ Forever"
52 Country with Mount Everest on its border
53 Caustic cleaners
54 Venomous vipers
55 Whack, as a fly
56 Frau's spouse
60 Peyton's brother on the gridiron
61 Lid

by Lynn Lempel

62 Repeated words
shouted after
"Who wants . . . ?"
63 Summer hrs. in D.C.

22 EASY

Note: The circled letters in this puzzle, when read in the correct order, spell the name of a shape. The four unclued answers are common three-word phrases usually accompanied by this shape.

ACROSS

1 Furniture on which a guest might sleep
5 Some 24-hr. breakfast places
10 Magician's word
14 Resting at night
15 Military academy enrollee
16 Leave out
17 [See note]
19 Toothpaste flavor
20 Marsh plant
21 Founding owner of the Pittsburgh Steelers
23 Powerful connections
25 Goofs
26 [See note]
32 Oriental, e.g.
33 Mount in Exodus
34 Pair of ___
38 Group of voters
40 Pair of ___
42 Lash
43 Food often eaten with chopsticks
45 Asian gambling mecca
47 Have bills
48 [See note]
51 Many a campaign event
54 "For ___ a jolly . . ."
55 Uncomfortable
59 Back in style
63 Chew (on)
64 [See note]
66 ___ Hari
67 Peace ___
68 Poe writing
69 Like volcanic fallout
70 "Laughing" creature
71 Black cat, to some

DOWN

1 "___ who?"
2 Double-reeded instrument
3 Long-term hostility
4 A little faster than largo
5 Word repeated before "Baby" in a hip-hop title
6 "Very funny"
7 River separating Germany and Poland
8 Flippantly cocky
9 Dual-track, in a way
10 Day when procrastination ends, supposedly
11 ___ acid (protein builder)
12 Eatery
13 Lawyers: Abbr.
18 Is a tenant
22 Some medals for Spanish athletes
24 The Titanic, e.g.
26 City, to Cicero
27 Original "Star Trek" helmsman
28 They may need boosting
29 As a friend, to François
30 Assaulted, in a way
31 Leave behind, informally
35 Cut of meat
36 New Zealander
37 Tore
39 Ruin bit by bit, with "at"
41 Pageant wrap
44 TV's "How ___ Your Mother"
46 Wombs
49 Sad sort
50 Familiar with
51 Summation symbol in math
52 They're below elbows
53 "The Colossus and Other Poems" poet
56 Sailor's call
57 Beget
58 Presenter of many game shows?
60 Jets or Nets
61 Reign
62 "Yes, we're ___"
65 Govt. insurer of seniors

by Milo Beckman

23 **EASY**

ACROSS

1 Late, as a library book
8 Sound of an excited heart
15 "-" marks
16 Furious
17 Surplus's opposite
18 Bring up, as a subject
19 Forget-me-___
20 Ruler on a golf course?
21 Yank
24 Floppy feature of a basset hound
26 "My country, ___ of thee"
27 Morales of "NYPD Blue"
28 In favor of
30 Mushroom cloud creator, briefly
34 Scrape, as a knee
35 Songwriter Berlin
37 "___ pasa?"
38 Little bell sound
39 Electron tube
40 Be furious
41 Rock music genre
42 Heart-shaped item on a chain, say
43 Genie's home
44 Last movement of a sonata
46 Tire filler
47 Stick ___ in the water

48 Atlantic food fish
50 Foreign policy grp.
52 Hawaii's state bird
53 Ruler in a vegetable garden?
56 Comic strip cry
58 Folded Mexican dish
59 Element used to make semiconductors
63 Not recognizable by
64 Raw material for a steel mill
65 Figure with 14-Down sides
66 Rainbow mnemonic

DOWN

1 Advanced deg.
2 Sailor's affirmative
3 Beach lotion letters
4 Ruler after a diet?
5 Art ___ (1920s–30s movement)
6 Join
7 Superlative suffix
8 Fine cotton
9 Like krypton
10 Ruler on a beach?
11 Easel user
12 Ache
13 Bug-eyed
14 Number of sides in a 65-Across
20 Ruler in a Utah city?
21 Court clown
22 Igloo builder

23 Spoil, as a parade
25 Zimbabwe's continent
29 Passengers
31 Consider the same
32 Order to come
33 Cone-shaped shelter
35 Bachelor's last words
36 Badminton court divider
40 Ruler with custard desserts?
42 Ruler in a W.C.?
45 Where many fed. employees live
49 "Me too"
51 Egypt's capital
53 Whine
54 Guitarist Clapton
55 Midday
57 Fill to excess
58 Rotten
59 Madam's mate
60 Corn on the ___
61 ". . . ___ quit!"
62 Las Vegas's home: Abbr.

by Michael David

ACROSS

1 With 10-Across and the circled letters, a best-selling novel, with "The"
5 Excavation find
10 See 1-Across
14 Environs
15 Musical exercise
16 Start of a legal memo
17 Heroine of 1-/10-Across, etc.
20 Ballpark fig.
21 It's found in stacks
22 One taking a gander?
23 Bygone muscle cars
24 The King's middle name
26 Horror film sound
29 Zero personality?
33 "___ is human"
34 Kipling's "___ Din"
35 Tango requirement
36 During
37 It's to your advantage
38 "Little piggies"
39 Actor Cariou
40 TV doctor Sanjay
41 Old photo tint
42 Silicon Valley city
44 1940s Bikini blasts, for short
45 Cause for calling in the National Guard
46 Takes to court
47 Not flighty
50 Lead-in to boy or girl
51 Has been
54 Hero of 1-/10-Across, etc.
58 God of war and magic
59 English Romantic poet William
60 Canal of song
61 Part of a pool
62 Author Larsson of 1-/10-Across, etc.
63 There's no "I" in it, they say

DOWN

1 Air force?
2 Rainbow goddess
3 Relaxation
4 Experimentation station
5 Seized again
6 Spirit of a people
7 One of the seven deadly sins
8 Gilbert and Sullivan princess
9 Cartoon frame
10 Actress Ryder
11 Prefix with China
12 Number of Los Lonely Boys
13 "Take this"
18 Fragrant compound
19 Public place in Athens
23 Encircle
24 Sleeper's problem
25 Armory grp.
26 Conk out
27 Prefix with -pathy
28 Ones holding their horses?
29 Boots
30 Some sports car features
31 "You ___ to yourself . . ."
32 Some Spanish flowers
34 "The ___ and Other Recent Discoveries About Human Sexuality" (1982 best seller)
37 Self starter?
38 Perturbs, with "off"
40 Dance movement
41 Porterhouse, for one
43 1906 Massenet opera based on Greek myth
44 Mace source
46 Feed, as a fire
47 Factor in an air-quality rating
48 Beach washer
49 Similar (to)
50 Jai ___
51 Something a police informant might wear
52 Where Indians live
53 Stern's opposite

by Adam G. Perl

55 Figure watchers'
   figs.
56 Deli order, for short
57 Animal doc

ACROSS

1 Fret
5 Singer/actress Midler
10 Heading on a list of errands
14 Memo
15 No turn may be allowed then, according to a sign
16 Lab assistant in a horror film
17 Face-to-face exam
18 Group that includes North, South, East and West
20 Actor Thornton of "Sling Blade"
22 Opposite of exits
23 Shower
24 ___ fide
25 Carlsbad feature
28 Chesapeake Bay delicacy
32 Beelike
33 Can of worms, say
34 Singer Yoko
35 Writer Ayn and others
36 Naval rank: Abbr.
37 Bare-bones
39 Frigid
40 Writing tablets
41 Dentist's directive
42 Activity a puppy loves
45 Talked back to
46 Currier and ___

47 Bit of bumper damage
48 Golden Delicious and others
51 Service provided at Meineke and Pep Boys
55 Sparring injury, perhaps
57 California wine valley
58 Bygone Italian coins
59 Artless
60 Hawaiian strings, informally
61 Ones giving or receiving alimony
62 Like some preppy jackets
63 Eat like a bird

DOWN

1 High-hatter
2 Spelling of "90210"
3 And others, for short
4 Versed in the classics, say
5 Certain spool
6 Company with a spectacular 2001 bankruptcy
7 Chicago daily, briefly, with "the"
8 Koppel or Kennedy
9 Just beat, as in a competition

10 Something always sold in mint condition?
11 Eye amorously
12 Sullen
13 Heavenly bodies
19 Feminine suffix
21 Tall tales
24 Seventh heaven
25 West Indies native
26 Rapidly
27 Old LPs and 45s
28 Quaint lodging hinted at by the outsides of 18-, 20-, 28-, 42-, 51- or 55-Across
29 Reddish/white horses
30 Biscotti flavoring
31 Like chicken breast cutlets
33 Boyfriends
37 Shenanigan
38 "Now hear this!"
40 Something brought to a birthday party
43 Easter blooms
44 Designer ___ Saint Laurent
45 Bottom of the ocean
47 The "D" of PRNDL
48 Competent
49 Grand ___ (auto race)
50 Chaste
51 Cheese popular with crackers

by Susan L. Stanislawski

52 Actor Gyllenhaal
53 Crude group?
54 Take in some sun
56 Black bird

ACROSS

1 Child prodigy of "Heroes"
6 Painters' degs.
10 "Pygmalion" playwright
14 "Falstaff" or "Fidelio"
15 "Play it, Sam" speaker
16 Bridgestone product
17 Package full of syringes?
19 Ancient Andean
20 Great Giant
21 Kardashian matriarch
22 Less likely to be carded, say
23 Thesis topic for sex ed?
26 Picture puzzles
29 Acorn or pecan
30 Berry for the health-conscious
31 Loudly berate
36 Cameras taking pictures of permanent markers?
40 Like some summer dresses, by design
41 "___ Enchanted" (2004 film)
42 Stimpy's TV pal
43 God, with "the"
46 Pompom on a skullcap?

51 Building blocks
52 It changes hands at an altar
53 Give a name
56 Cookie celebrating its centennial in 2012
57 Police investigation of a betting house?
60 Pig's sound
61 Jiffy ___
62 Students take them in class
63 Dogs, cats and gerbils
64 "South Park" writer Parker
65 Put out, as energy

DOWN

1 It's stolen in an Austin Powers movie
2 "___ a Spell on You"
3 Penny
4 Noah's vessel
5 17-syllable poems
6 Makes like
7 Item "spirited" past security?
8 "Do ___ do"
9 "My gal" of song
10 One of a pair for a clown
11 Bangalore believer, maybe
12 See 46-Down
13 Tired

18 ___ Lackawanna Railroad
22 Bone: Prefix
23 Peculiarity
24 Go slowly (along)
25 Multinational currency
26 Speak with a scratchy voice
27 It comes back to you
28 False deity
31 Fast jet, for short
32 Troubled terribly
33 Tuna ___
34 Singer Guthrie
35 Romanov ruler
37 "Midnight in ___" (2011 Woody Allen film)
38 Notion: Fr.
39 Ages and ages
43 "Holy smokes!"
44 Rice-A-___
45 Oregon city
46 Short baseball hit that's 12-Down
47 Spooky
48 Go-between
49 Cozy spots
50 Look into
53 Information on a check
54 Consumer
55 Outdo
57 Sandwich usually served with mayo

by Zoe Wheeler and Aimee Lucido

58 "___ Mutual Friend"
(Dickens's last
finished novel)
59 Actress Courteney

ACROSS

1 Shaggy's nickname for his canine friend
6 Winnie-the-___
10 Did cartoons, e.g.
14 "A Fish Called ___"
15 The "A" in A.D.
16 Letter before kappa
17 Less friendly
18 Mexican money
19 Hgts.
20 Rapper who came to prominence as a member of the Wu-Tang Clan
23 Karate teacher
24 Pianist's practice piece
25 Former Republican-turned-Democratic senator from Pennsylvania
30 Blouse undergarment
33 Suffix with absorb
34 Skylit rooms
35 Little 'uns
38 Mouths, slangily
40 Neither this nor that
41 104, in old Rome
42 "You betcha!"
43 Form of sparring
48 Golf legend Sam
49 Kitt who sang "Santa Baby"
53 Whiskey or vodka
57 Tulsa's home: Abbr.
58 Potpourri
59 Intends (to)
60 ___ moss
61 Dispatched
62 Skip over, as a vowel
63 Roof overhang
64 Focus for an arborist
65 Screenwriter Ephron

DOWN

1 Drinks from a flask, say
2 Storage for fast Web page retrieval
3 "America's Finest News Source," with "The"
4 Ukrainian port whose staircase is a setting for "The Battleship Potemkin"
5 Trade
6 "Come to ___"
7 Words below the Lincoln Memorial
8 Beginnings
9 Begin a tryst
10 Language offshoots
11 Go round and round
12 Blues singer James
13 Laundry
21 ___-O-Fish (McDonald's sandwich)
22 Outputs of brainstorming
26 Nav. rank
27 Deuce topper
28 What Dubliners call their homeland
29 Speak with laryngitis, say
30 Homies
31 Hitter of 714 home runs
32 Ottoman official
36 It leans to the right
37 Rice-___
38 "Kid-tested, mother-approved" cereal
39 Brown, Dartmouth, etc.
41 Opiate often used in cough syrup
44 Lament of the defeated
45 One playing hoops
46 Snoozed
47 Cover on the front of a car
50 One might be made of bread crumbs
51 Language of India
52 Confused
53 Extraordinary, in slang
54 European-based furniture giant
55 Bulgarian or Czech
56 Focus lovingly (on)

by Guy Tabachnick

28 EASY

ACROSS

1 Cornered
6 "Quiet!"
11 Program abbr.
14 Prop up
15 Canned pumpkin, e.g.
16 Spot for a band
17 Winner of a pea-preparing contest?
19 Maker of the Soul and Optima
20 Figure skating jump
21 Shoemaker's tool
22 Portents
24 Hypotheticals
26 Names on fake IDs, perhaps
28 Lotharios' lines in a singles bar?
33 Waxed enthusiastic, say
34 "Neato!"
35 "___, Brute?"
38 Cause of some weaving, for short
39 Early TV star with a biography titled "Schnozzola"
42 Western alliance, for short
43 Build up a nest egg
45 Desertlike
46 Store featured in "Miracle on 34th Street"

48 One preparing corn for long hours?
51 Prince who married Kate Middleton
53 F1 neighbor on a PC
54 Bird with prized plumes
55 Measure of electrical resistance
57 Campus near Beverly Hills, briefly
61 U.N. agency for workers
62 Phony wedding?
66 Gehrig on the diamond
67 Take the lid off
68 Commandeer
69 The "L" in 57-Across
70 Past its sell-by date
71 Tree with a namesake ski destination

DOWN

1 Group whose music is heard in "Mamma Mia!"
2 Fearsome dino
3 First, second, third or home
4 Mimic
5 "You're right!"
6 Gush
7 Ship's framework
8 Virtual address
9 Meet with
10 Valiant

11 Assesses one's options carefully
12 Pickling solution
13 Accumulate
18 Barn door fastener
23 Fabricate
25 Elmer with a big gun
26 Makes up (for)
27 Light, rhythmic cadence
28 Seed containers
29 Early stop in a presidential race
30 Gallant
31 Edvard Munch depiction
32 White with age
36 "Rent" actor Diggs
37 Old NATO target
40 Fed. agency entrusted with food safety
41 Outback sprinters
44 Magazine whose name sounds like a letter of the alphabet
47 Charges in court
49 It turns red in acid
50 Spheric opener?
51 Kurt who wrote the music for "The Threepenny Opera"
52 Domed home
55 Like the Sabin polio vaccine

by Lynn Lempel

ACROSS

1 Money owed
5 Lamebrain
9 Nukes
13 Good, as a driver's license
15 Addict
16 Replacement for the mark, franc and lira
17 Pilotless plane
18 "___ closed!"
19 Opera solo
20 Impatiently endure passing time
23 Hoopla
25 "Have something!"
26 Outback bird
27 Hi-___ monitor
28 Win by enough points, in sports gambling
32 Big-jawed dinosaur, for short
33 Erie Canal mule
34 No. on a business card
35 Brand of kitchen wrap
37 Rug rat
39 Hits with a fist
43 One of the Three Stooges
45 Friend
47 Grammy winner from County Donegal, Ireland
48 Perform a routine household chore
52 Dispirited
53 Post-op area
54 "___ Abner"
55 Line of Canon cameras
56 Pass through a crisis safely
60 Where the Himalayas are
61 Tied, as a score
62 Egypt's Sadat
65 Craft in which to go down a river, say
66 Part to play
67 Get ready to sing the national anthem
68 Monotonous routines
69 Concordes, for short
70 Roget offerings (abbr.) . . . or, loosely, the first and last words of 20-, 28-, 48- and 56-Across

DOWN

1 Netflix rental
2 Big part of a hare
3 Pass without effect, as a storm
4 Funny Fey
5 So
6 "Time ___ a premium"
7 Fits with another, as a gear tooth
8 Forestall by acting first
9 Fervor
10 ___ borealis
11 Having a store tag
12 Long baths
14 Hinder
21 Lions and tigers
22 Medical successes
23 Each of Shakespeare's plays has five
24 Nickelodeon's "___ the Explorer"
29 Tests
30 Have a nontraditional marriage, in a way
31 Talk show host DeGeneres
36 Like a perfect game in baseball
38 Some brewskis
40 In progress
41 Greek sandwich
42 Utters
44 Crystal trophy inscribers, e.g.
46 Where a lion hides
48 Onetime Wisconsin-based insurance giant
49 Directionless at sea
50 Spanish eggs
51 Radii neighbors
52 Ringo who sang "Yellow Submarine"
57 D.C. team, informally
58 Hibernian, for one
59 Tolkien's talking tree race
63 The Beach Boys' "Barbara ___"
64 Hwys.

by John Dunn

ACROSS
1 "Kinsman" of Tarzan
4 Impact sound
8 Spicy cuisine
13 A witch might put one on you
14 Just about forever
15 Epoch when mammals arose
16 Klee contemporary
17 Monte Cristo ingredient
19 Sharon of "Cagney & Lacey"
21 Old Saturn model
22 Scholar's deg.
23 Spelling aid?
26 Church bells' sound
27 Get in a row
28 Response at the altar
29 Mesa ___ National Park
30 Sharon of "Valley of the Dolls"
31 Club ___
32 Tightened up
33 Pub hub
36 Legally impedes
39 Math subj.
40 Commando weapons
44 Teakettle feature
45 Ga. neighbor
46 Secluded valleys
47 Stretched to the max
48 Where people are always putting things?

50 Those aboard a U.F.O.
51 "___ semper tyrannis"
52 Swab the floor again
53 Like 17-, 23-, 33- and 48-Across
57 Aegean island on which Homer is said to be buried
59 N.Y. Yankees' division
60 Castle obstacle
61 Big D.C. lobby
62 Gymnast Comaneci
63 John's other half
64 Car that "really drives 'em wi-i-ild," in a 1960s song

DOWN
1 Inventor's cry
2 Vine-covered passageway
3 Heroic deed
4 Oil name
5 "In what way?"
6 "Gimme ___!" (start of an Illinois cheer)
7 Ed.'s stack
8 Harry who co-founded Columbia Pictures
9 Server's wish
10 "Golly!"
11 Expose to light
12 Ribbed
15 Green sci.

18 Storage site
20 Beat by a nose
23 Fermenting locale
24 Nuts, berries, etc., for squirrels
25 Kook
26 Tick-tock maker
29 Part of a chapter: Abbr.
31 ___ Butterworth
32 It may put someone out
34 Likely
35 Norwegian king
36 Grammy-winning Gloria
37 Burger flipper
38 A bit messy, as the hair
41 Closing (in on)
42 Playfully
43 Montreal-to-Boston dir.
45 Nina of 1940s–50s films
46 Attends
48 Natural talent
49 Haunted house sound
51 Slugger Sammy
54 China's Chou En-___
55 "Peg ___ Heart"
56 Stall in London
58 ___ Tomé

by Susan Gelfand

ACROSS

1 Mix with a spoon
5 Not go
9 Political science subj.
13 Biblical water-to-wine locale
14 Snapshot
15 Flightless bird of South America
16 "Incidentally . . ."
18 Performs in a play
19 Response of sympathy
20 Suffix with ranch
21 Cozy dining spot
22 Lone Star State
23 Beef jerky brand
25 Egg-hatching spot
27 Filmmaker with style and total control
30 Pairs
33 ___ Hoop
36 1968 A.L. M.V.P. and Cy Young winner ___ McLain
37 Cigarette's end
38 "Holy cow!"
40 Dedicated poem
41 Striped equine
43 Suspect, in cop lingo
44 Pairs
45 Goofs
47 Carve into, as a plaque
49 Performing in a play, say
52 Following the law
56 Skating jump
58 Sony rival
59 Southwest desert that includes Death Valley
60 Sound heard in an empty hallway
61 "Never mind"
63 Secluded valley
64 Like much diet food, informally
65 1970 Kinks hit
66 Indian woman's attire
67 Found's opposite
68 Rear end

DOWN

1 Sir Walter who wrote "Ivanhoe"
2 Western lake near Squaw Valley
3 E-mail folder
4 Some stylish sunglasses
5 Pronoun for a ship
6 Locker room handout
7 Big name in arcade games
8 Chinese-American virtuoso cellist
9 Rock associated with hardness
10 "Let's be serious here . . ."
11 Presidential rejection
12 Chore
14 Deg. for a prof
17 Zap with a stun gun
23 A lumberjack might leave one behind
24 "Knocked Up" director Apatow
26 Sound heard in a movie theater
28 Loosen, as laces
29 Some whiskeys
30 Flabbergasted state
31 Consumer
32 "You've gotta be joking!"
34 Chemical in drain cleaners
35 Have a meeting of the minds
38 Rowers
39 Withdraw, with "out"
42 Packaged pasta brand
44 2011 Oscar-nominated film about African-American maids
46 Leisurely walk
48 Drain cleaner target
50 Sound heard before "Gesundheit!"
51 Large fishing hooks
53 Swamp critter
54 Walled city in Spain
55 Allow to attack
56 Pants fillers
57 The Bruins of the N.C.A.A.

by Ian Livengood

59 Muscular actor with a mohawk

62 Grain in Cheerios

ACROSS

1 Insecticide whose spelled-out name has 31 letters
4 Rapid, in music
9 Film about a statue?
15 Always, in verse
16 Woolf's "___ of One's Own"
17 Hard-to-hum, say
18 2004 movie with a screenplay by Tina Fey
20 Japanese mat
21 Was next to
22 ___ Noël (French Santa Claus)
23 Straight, at a bar
24 Carved figure used for rituals
29 Lees material
31 Legal wrongs
32 How a limbo dancer dances
33 "___ chance!"
36 N.Y.C.'s Roosevelt ___
37 Railroad beam
38 Work by Sir Edward Elgar hinted at by this puzzle's shaded squares
44 Like most of China's flag
45 Fig. on an A.T.M. receipt
46 Improperly off base, in brief

47 "Wise" bird
48 Like the cutouts in some children's artwork
50 Austrian-made pistol
54 Industrial Revolution-era power source
58 "Dies ___"
59 Bit of Highlands costume
60 Illicit rendezvous locale
62 Yacht site
65 Family play time
66 2,000 pounds
67 It's taken by witnesses
68 Try to stop from squeaking, say
69 Chicken
70 Trials
71 SSW's opposite

DOWN

1 Supply's partner, in economics
2 Pundit Myers
3 Roman emperor born in Spain
4 Nativity scene figures
5 Part of an airtight seal
6 More achy
7 Stravinsky's "L'Histoire du ___"
8 Meditation chants

9 Intellectual property subject
10 2600 and 5200 consoles
11 Figure on a pole
12 ___ while
13 '60s war zone
14 Clay, after a transformation?
19 Mentioning
22 Xerxes' empire
25 ___ dire (jury selection process)
26 Choir voice
27 Enter
28 Milk providers
30 May honoree
34 Plateau
35 "___, and quit my sight!": Macbeth
38 Love god
39 Wetlands creature
40 Empty, as talk
41 "Break ___!"
42 Dress (up)
43 Urbana-Champaign athletes
48 Key of Mozart's Symphony No. 25 or 40
49 Grow, as a pupil
51 Terminus of a famous trail
52 Collect one's winnings
53 One whistling in the kitchen?
55 Japanese dog

by Kyle T. Dolan

56 Enrique's "Enough!"
57 News conference, e.g.
61 Terminates
62 Comfy bit of footwear
63 Enero-to-diciembre period
64 Button with two triangles: Abbr.
65 Astronomical observation std.

ACROSS

1 Suffix with differ
4 Early American patriot Thomas
9 Speedy
14 Gen ___ (child of a 29-Across)
15 Capital of Jordan
16 "William Tell," for one
17 Where: Lat.
18 Land that's not inland
19 Gave a speeding ticket
20 Stereotypical entree at a campaign event
23 It's transfused in a transfusion
24 Brits' thank-yous
25 ___ carte
28 Powerful D.C. lobby
29 One born in the late 1940s or '50s
33 Prefix with conservative
34 ___-Japanese War
35 Lerner's songwriting partner
36 Item carried by an Amish driver
39 Way underpriced
42 Ogled
43 Nothing ___ the truth
46 Farmer's wish
49 10th grader: Abbr.
50 ___-Caps
51 Cheerleader's cheer
52 Authored
53 The starts of 20-, 29-, 36- and 46-Across, e.g., when repeated quickly in order
58 Protein acid, for short
60 U.C.L.A. athlete
61 "If you ask me," in texts
62 Sainted ninth-century pope
63 Daily reading for a pope
64 Clean air org.
65 Orange soda brand
66 "Sailing to Byzantium" poet
67 Roll of green?

DOWN

1 Beyond the metro area
2 Interstellar clouds
3 ___ Bridge (former name of New York's R.F.K. Bridge)
4 Walked back and forth
5 Love personified
6 Apple computer
7 Poet Ogden
8 Thing
9 Absolutely dependable
10 ". . . blackbirds baked in ___"
11 Honeybunch or snookums
12 Rage
13 Annual June honoree
21 Jazz style
22 Taxi
26 ___ Alcindor (Kareem Abdul-Jabbar, once)
27 Live and breathe
29 Gargantuan
30 Taiwanese-born director Lee
31 Charles of "Algiers," 1938
32 "Alley ___!"
34 Luminous stellar explosion
36 Protestant denom.
37 Cheyenne's home: Abbr.
38 Cool, in old slang
39 "___ News Sunday Morning"
40 Attila, for one
41 Love or rage
43 Wee 'un's footwear
44 Lively, in music
45 In phrases, something to share or hit
47 Dishcloth
48 A little on the heavy side
49 12th graders: Abbr.
52 Rosés, e.g.
54 "I'm ___!"
55 Great Lake between Huron and Ontario

by Kurt Mueller

56 Heavy instrument to march with

57 Lose freshness, as a flower

58 1936 candidate Landon

59 ___ culpa

The circles in this puzzle are contained in words that form a sequence. Connect these circles, in the order of the sequence, to form an appropriate image.

ACROSS

1 Grooms groom it
4 High beams
11 Price in cents of a 1958 Monroe stamp
16 ... of a 1968 Jefferson stamp
17 Went berserk
18 ... of a 1938 Jackson stamp
19 ___ Arizona (Pearl Harbor memorial)
20 Caterpillar part
21 Correct
22 Shared quarters (with)
24 Laura of "Jurassic Park"
26 Fine ___
27 Chef's subject
30 Guinness, e.g.
32 Do some logrolling
33 Hall-of-Famer Mel
35 "Come on in!"
39 Location for some quick calculations
43 Sanctifies
44 ... of a 1903 Washington stamp
45 They might precede "Monsieur!"
46 Funny stuff
48 Low-ranking officers
51 Crumbly cheese
54 In ___ (dazed)
56 Chihuahua, e.g.
58 "Ni-i-ice!"
60 Circus performer
63 Author LeShan
64 Barn toppers
65 Refrain syllables
66 Hi-___ graphics
67 "Family Ties" mother
68 Sexy nightwear
69 ... of a 1970 Eisenhower stamp

DOWN

1 ... of a 1954 Lincoln stamp
2 Not mixing well
3 Tapped asset
4 Bonny hillsides
5 The Amazing ___
6 Bank earnings: Abbr.
7 Aspiring Ph.D.'s test
8 Rear
9 Colorations
10 Begin to berate
11 Org. doing pat-downs
12 Study of blood
13 Camper driver, for short
14 Med. specialty
15 Gridiron positions
23 Ice cream drinks
25 Angry parent's decree, maybe
28 "Where do you think you're going?!"
29 Archaic verb suffix
31 "It's no ___!"
32 Consumer protection org.
34 Asian celebration
36 Quarter ___ (McDonald's orders)
37 "The Phantom Menace," in the "Star Wars" series
38 Super ___ (game console)
40 The Cowboys of the Big 12 Conf.
41 Disaster relief acronym
42 Lamb suckler
47 Swiss pharmaceutical giant
49 Played out
50 Minute bits
51 ... of a 1964 Kennedy stamp
52 Tel Aviv lander
53 Pint-size
55 Tassel sporter
57 Beano alternative
59 Suffix with Taiwan
61 Bygone
62 Actress ___ Ling of "The Crow"

by Daniel A. Finan

35 EASY

ACROSS
1 Stick in one's ___
5 Czech capital
11 Banned organic compound, for short
14 TV's warrior princess
15 Compassionate
16 Kind of baseball or battery
17 A classic beauty who is not all there
19 Satellite-based navigation aid, in brief
20 That is, in Latin
21 Plains tribe
22 Wrap worn in India
23 Broadcast
25 Mini-hospital
27 Booster of the Apollo space program
33 Frigid
34 Younger brother of Cain and Abel
35 Lowest point
39 Country on the south side of Mount Everest
42 Chinese philosopher ___-tzu
43 Lopez with the 1963 hit "If I Had a Hammer"
44 Spanish artist El ___
45 Colored part of the eye

47 Lead-in to maniac or surfing
48 1960s–70s Ford Company model
52 Microscopic blob
55 West Coast travel hub, informally
56 "Largemouth" fish
57 By way of
60 Number in an octet
64 Many a line on a flight route map
65 Milky Way bars and others
68 With 53-Down, a coffee-flavored liqueur
69 Some marbles
70 Book before Nehemiah
71 Floppy rabbit feature
72 Refuses to acknowledge
73 River across the French/German border

DOWN
1 116, in ancient Rome
2 Clarinet or sax
3 Actress Hathaway
4 Wisconsin city
5 What an M.A. might go on to earn
6 Regret
7 Bullets, informally
8 Walk or trot

9 Open with a key
10 Fairness-in-hiring inits.
11 Polytheistic
12 Blue Grotto's island
13 Fundamental
18 Use a swizzle stick
22 Indian instrument
24 E.R. workers
26 Period after Shrove Tuesday
27 Be in a 32-Down, e.g.
28 Taiwan-based computer giant
29 Genre
30 Archaeologist's find
31 Japanese port
32 Group in church robes
36 "Carpe ___"
37 Playwright William
38 Hilarious one
40 High points
41 Richard ___, Clarence Darrow defendant
46 Word part: Abbr.
49 Wreak havoc on
50 Battle of Normandy city
51 Rust and lime
52 Diminish
53 See 68-Across
54 ___ the Grouch
58 Modern Persia
59 Italian wine city

by John R. O'Brien

61 Egyptian pyramid city

62 Wife of Zeus

63 Old Russian despot

65 "What, me worry?" magazine

66 So-so grade

67 Donkey

ACROSS

1 Add zip to, with "up"
6 Island north of Australia
11 Deserving detention, say
14 Maritime raptors
15 Farsi speaker
16 Suffix with glob
17 Boring predicaments?
19 C.F.O.'s deg., perhaps
20 Market researcher
21 Keep from practicing
23 Wet behind the ears
24 Defense acronym
27 Nick of "Warrior"
28 Tulip planters, perhaps?
31 "I got ___ in Kalamazoo"
33 Wrestling's Flair
34 Sci-fi sidekick, maybe
35 Strong advocates of margarine?
40 Classified ad inits.
41 Wet behind the ears
42 Sources of vitamin C
43 Bring Ebert and Moore together?
48 When brunch may be served
49 Art school subj.
50 Poker champ Ungar
53 "We're on!"
55 Nose-in-the-air

58 Blistex target
59 Expert ladder climbers?
62 Subgenre of punk
63 Hyundai model
64 One of Israel's 12
65 Police dept. rank
66 Wear black, say
67 "So ___ to offend . . ."

DOWN

1 It's bigger than a coupe
2 Kind of danish
3 Cause of many a family feud
4 Unit in a block
5 Catch sight of
6 "Get a bang out of life!" mint
7 Perturb
8 Prefix with content
9 Linear, for short
10 On the upturn
11 Big collector of pollen
12 Burden, figuratively
13 Sweetie pie
18 Word of denial
22 Get completely wet, in dialect
25 Donned hastily
26 Valhalla V.I.P.
28 Brooklynese pronoun
29 Final: Abbr.
30 Bump off

31 "Finally!"
32 Celebrity's talk show appearance, say
36 Goof up
37 ___ avis
38 Scratch up
39 Passports, e.g., in brief
40 Sent with a click
44 ___ Party
45 Memory trace
46 Certain meter reader
47 "At Last" singer James
50 Yarn purchase
51 Engine type
52 Like some stomachs and elections
54 Liqueur similar to Sambuca
56 Racket org.
57 N.F.L. snappers: Abbr.
60 Opposite of old, in Germany
61 [I'm mad!]

1	2	3	4	5	■	6	7	8	9	10	■	11	12	13
14					■	15					■	16		
17					18						■	19		
20						■	■		21		22			
23			■	■	24		25	26	■	27				
■	■	■	28	29					30					
■	31	32			■	■		33			■		34	
■	35				36	37				38	39			■
40			■	■	41			■	■	42			■	■
43			44	45			■	46	47			■	■	■
48					■	49				■	■	50	51	52
53				54		■	■	55		56	57			
58			■	59		60	61							
62			■	63				■	■	64				
65			■	66				■	■	67				

by Sharon Delorme

37 EASY

ACROSS

1 Chews the fat
5 Fiona, e.g., in "Shrek"
11 Hula-Hoops or Furbys, once
14 500 sheets of paper
15 Geronimo's tribe
16 Fury
17 Hankering
18 One knocked off a pedestal
20 Pasture
22 Course guide?
23 C.E.O.'s job: Abbr.
24 Paid postgraduate position at a university
27 Black-eyed ___
28 Cry after hitting a hammer on one's thumb, say
29 Morocco's capital
31 "Much ___ About Nothing"
34 Uncooked
36 Beethoven's "Für ___"
39 Solve a crossword, e.g.?
44 Greeted and seated
45 ___-lacto-vegetarian
46 Old Navy alternative
47 Harnessed, as oxen
50 Mother of Don Juan
53 "You said it, sister!"
55 Put a spade atop a spade, say
60 Barn dance seat
61 Miami locale: Abbr.
62 Cake words in "Alice in Wonderland"
63 Illegal wrestling hold
67 Newswoman Paula
68 "___ You Experienced" (Jimi Hendrix's first album)
69 Sean who wrote "Juno and the Paycock"
70 Like show horses' feet
71 Tavern
72 Walked purposefully
73 Tiny hill dwellers

DOWN

1 Harsh and brusque
2 Eaglet's nest
3 Breakfast order with a hole in it
4 Like gym socks
5 Dunderhead
6 4.0 is a great one: Abbr.
7 Kramden of "The Honeymooners"
8 Cream-filled pastry
9 Mount Everest guide
10 McCain or McConnell: Abbr.
11 Squirming
12 Kitchen magnet?
13 Shoulder muscles, for short
19 African antelope or Chevrolet
21 Jane or John in court
25 Threadbare
26 Hit, as a fly
30 ___ Paese cheese
31 C.I.O.'s partner
32 Repeated cry when sticking a stake in a vampire
33 1957 Disney dog movie
35 "___ Let the Dogs Out"
37 Cousin of calypso
38 Mind reading, for short
40 Big name in toy trains
41 Tattoos, slangily
42 Dastardly
43 Pro ___ (like some law work)
48 Cause's partner
49 Avis rival
51 Ram's mate
52 One of the Gabor sisters
53 Beeb comedy
54 Actress Tierney of "ER"
56 Catch, as a dogie
57 Salt Lake City native

by Andrea Carla Michaels and Michael Blake

58 "Can we turn on a
fan or something?!"
59 Manages, as a
71-Across

64 Denials
65 Brit. reference
work
66 Bill the Science Guy

38 EASY

ACROSS

1 "Th-that's cold!"
4 Humorist Barry
8 Exclaim using four-letter words
13 Richard ___ (anonymous name in court cases)
14 Outfielder Tommie of the Miracle Mets
15 Batter
17 "Et" translated
18 Ruthless figure in "The Godfather"
20 Time of little advancement
22 Rain-soaked dirt
23 East Coast state: Abbr.
24 Drop-___
25 First part of a 1952 best seller's title, followed by 37- and 51-Across
28 Obsidian rock producer
30 Rex Harrison's singer/actor son
31 Detail on a map
32 "Fax" prefix
34 Illegally take, old-style
36 Ladies' patriotic org.
37 More of the book title
39 Attorney's "thing"
42 Ray Charles hit of 1963
43 Ingres or Renoir
45 Verger on adolescence, informally
48 Evoking a "ho-hum"
50 Riata, e.g.
51 Rest of the book title
53 Utter jerk, rudely
54 N.M.-to-N.J. dir.
55 Square peg ___ round hole
56 Total dive, say
60 Husband-and-wife milestone
63 Ring leader?
64 One hoping to get a pass?
65 Universally known symbol
66 Giant tub
67 Howls with laughter
68 Italian "well"
69 Toronto's prov.

DOWN

1 With 59-Down, star of the work revealed by the first letters of the Across clues, which hint at this puzzle's theme
2 Novelist Jaffe
3 1948 John Wayne western
4 Babies' pops
5 Wide-eyed
6 Rome's Via ___
7 Onetime overseas trade grp.
8 Hedge component
9 1960 Elia Kazan film
10 Season under le soleil
11 Squabbling
12 Fail to do as promised
16 Sublease
19 Denver ___
21 Wood knot
26 Designer Carolina ___
27 Suffix with Benedict
28 Inc., overseas
29 "I got it!"
30 Porto-___ (capital of Benin)
33 It's "wider than a mile," in an old song
35 Queequeg's captain
38 Tom Clancy's ___ (2008 video game)
39 1959 John Wayne western
40 Frequently debunked ability
41 Sault ___ Marie
42 Born, in France
44 Moderate pace
45 Ice cream or candy
46 Champion
47 "Still . . ."
49 Shooting star?
52 Miniskirts reveal them
53 Songwriter Jule

by Peter A. Collins

57 Schoenberg's "Moses und ___"
58 Author Paton
59 See 1-Down

61 "Ain't ___ shame?!"
62 Many a recipient of hand-me-downs, informally

ACROSS

1 Piquancy
5 Feel in one's ___
8 Sycophants, slangily
15 1/12 of a ruler
16 Durham sch.
17 South Pacific region
18 Nebraska tribe
19 "___ Beso" (Paul Anka hit)
20 1970 song with the lyric "Whisper words of wisdom"
21 1965 song with the lyric "Isn't he a bit like you and me?"
24 Wealthy Brits
25 Fictitious
26 Chow down
28 1969 song with the lyric "Once there was a way to get back homeward"
33 Common people
34 Lament loudly
35 Sick
37 Singer DiFranco
38 1965 song with the lyric "These are words that go together well"
42 Low island
43 Election mo.
44 "Am ___ late?"
45 Heredity unit

46 1965 song with the lyric "Think of what you're saying"
52 Bear: Sp.
53 Nebraska neighbor
54 McCarthy-era attorney Roy
57 1968 song with the lyric "We all want to change the world"
61 1968 song with the lyric "Remember to let her into your heart"
64 Suffix with zinc
65 "Amos 'n' ___"
66 Candid, as a photo
67 Pecan or cashew
68 Some HDTV screens
69 Slip-ups
70 Car rte. displayer
71 Comfort

DOWN

1 Jewish homeland
2 Inner: Prefix
3 Garbage boat
4 One of filmdom's Avengers
5 "C'est la ___"
6 Invisible
7 Cartoonist Nast
8 German cathedral city
9 Cold cube
10 Sink, as the sun
11 Jeanne d'Arc, e.g.
12 "Do ___ others . . ."
13 Mr. ___ (soft drink)

14 Mailing encls.
22 Conclusion
23 "For ___ know . . ."
26 Disney's "___ and the Detectives"
27 Up to the task
28 First Moody Blues hit
29 Martini garnish
30 Delta competitor: Abbr.
31 Houston sch.
32 Bias
33 Enthusiast
36 Soapmaking stuff
38 Unaccounted-for G.I.'s
39 "Pay ___ mind"
40 Mooer
41 Physicist with a law
45 Lose freshness
47 Scam
48 Stark ___ mad
49 Get tense and hard, as a muscle
50 Archipelago bits
51 Letter after sigma
54 Common bait fish
55 Wine: Prefix
56 Syringe, for short
57 Cherry and ruby
58 Ancient Peruvian
59 Bookies give them
60 Big Board inits.
62 Troop-entertaining grp.
63 "In excelsis ___"

by Peter A. Collins

ACROSS

1 "Don't say it!"
5 "Don't tase me, ___!"
8 Like traditional movies, for short
12 Othello, e.g.
13 Hardly a natty dresser
14 Rude sorts
15 Not esto or eso
16 Home of the Rockies: Abbr.
17 Last movement of a sonata
18 Traditional
20 Four Holy Roman emperors
21 Guest passes
22 Boiling
23 Jolly Green Giant's outburst
26 ___ dragon
29 Treasure in un castillo
30 Singer Donny or Marie
33 "The Pearl of ___ Island" (Harriet Beecher Stowe novel)
35 Spills (over)
37 Madrid zoo attraction
38 Stage item accompanying many a stand-up comic
39 Somewhat, in music
40 Main thoroughfare through N.Y.C.'s Chinatown
42 1969 "bed-in" participant
43 Orbiter of Mars
45 Intro material
47 Blue
48 Didn't fall
50 Turn up one's nose at
53 "Still a G Thang" rapper
57 Against the rules
58 Catchy musical phrase
59 Booty
60 Spanish skating figures
61 Ones taking night flights?
62 Vision: Prefix
63 Film set item
64 C.I.A. forerunner
65 General ___ chicken

DOWN

1 Sequel to "Typee"
2 Wilson's "The ___ Baltimore"
3 Away from L'Antarctique
4 Jesse who pitched a major-league record 1,252 games
5 Arcing hit
6 Chocolatey Hershey candy
7 Ancient Greek coin
8 [Out of my way!]
9 Refuses to
10 Great Seal word
11 U.K. decorations
13 Stupid sorts
14 Stick between the legs?
19 Some salmon
22 Brick carrier
23 Ambulance's destination: Abbr.
24 Lowest deck of a ship
25 Moonshine
26 Part of a tied tie
27 Reason for a bib
28 Maine university town
31 Things Old MacDonald hears
32 Düsseldorf-to-Dresden direction
34 Trudge
36 Place for a break
38 It makes a cutting edge
40 Cut (down)
41 Spies, slangily
44 Knocks on the noggin
46 Certain stock sale
48 Fools but good
49 Ax and adz
50 One not socializing much with hoi polloi

by Steve Riley

51 Conan O'Brien's Team ___
52 Roman emperor of A.D. 69
53 "Git!"
54 Boo-boo follower
55 Attend
56 Classic muscle cars

41 MEDIUM

When this puzzle is completed, the 10 circled letters, read from top to bottom, will spell a name associated with 39-Across.

ACROSS

1 *Peddle
5 Prefix with "mom" in 2009 news
9 Bay State sch.
14 Tommie of the Miracle Mets
15 *Christmas carol starter
16 Soil enricher
17 Gorillas and others
19 Manhattan's ___ Place
20 "No joke!," with "I'm"
22 *Storied also-ran
23 January 1 sound
26 Intersected
27 Grapefruit choice
29 *Managed ___
31 Coeur d'___
33 Vietnam-era protest org.
34 Potentially Q.E.D.-worthy
37 Article in rap titles
39 Classic novel of 1,000+ pages . . . or a hint to the word ladder formed by the answers to the starred clues
42 Columnist Hentoff
43 Earring shape
46 45 ___
49 Contrarian's retort
51 *Center
52 Brown in the funnies

54 Best Buy buys
57 "___ who?"
58 *Place to moor
59 "Give me an example!"
62 Oscar winner Tatum
64 "You're fired!" speaker, informally
68 Slowly, on a score
69 *Valentine sentiment
70 "___ it my way"
71 Test for quality
72 River of Flanders
73 *Chocolate brand

DOWN

1 Broomstick rider
2 Cabinet dept.
3 Elfin
4 New Zealand parrots
5 Midway Airport alternative
6 Napoleonic leader?
7 Palm product
8 "Why not?!"
9 Thurman of "In Bloom"
10 Overly romantic
11 Places for rites
12 Wrote for an orchestra
13 Tatters
18 Pro ___ (for now)
21 Drink brewed naturally
23 Angel dust
24 Item in a thole
25 Ship's christening spot

28 Joy of "The View"
30 Olympic skating champion Lysacek
32 Resulted in
35 Run out of town on ___
36 Drives home, as runs
38 "Back in Black" band
40 Personal bugaboo
41 Bow-toting god
44 Prospector's find
45 Brand of movable collectibles
46 Soda brand since 1905
47 7-Down and others
48 Whizzes
50 Without muss or fuss
53 Ranch in "Giant"
55 Java or C++ whiz
56 Hostess ___ Balls
60 Units now called siemens
61 Queen Wheat City of Oklahoma
63 Myrna of film
65 Hubbub
66 Tyler of "Jersey Girl"
67 Presidential monogram

by Elizabeth C. Gorski

ACROSS

1 Nursery rhyme vessel
5 Candy used to be seen on it
9 Like a celestial body
14 Oscar Wilde poem "By the ___"
15 Ingredient in traditional medicine
16 Uncertain
17 Start of a Confucian aphorism
20 Man's name that's Latin for "honey"
21 Not so great
22 Arm raiser, informally
23 Like the gang, in an old song
25 Single, e.g.
28 Accept eagerly, with "up"
29 A goner
31 Dig it
32 Work assignments
35 TV network that broadcast live from Opryland USA
36 Two-time Oscar-winning cinematographer Nykvist
37 Aphorism's middle
40 Draftable
41 Tick off
42 Journalist Howell
43 Actor Wheaton
44 Medgar ___ College
46 Number twos, for short
47 Some galas
49 Accustoms
53 Place for family portraits
54 Together, in Toulon
55 Suffix with manager
56 Aphorism's end
60 Beau
61 Call ___ (stop play after service)
62 "Am ___ only one?"
63 Terminals in a computer network
64 Minuscule issues
65 Word with china or chop

DOWN

1 Cheese city
2 Staggering
3 Probably
4 Joke follower
5 Not being such a daredevil, say
6 Place for many a hanging
7 Brings along
8 Speed: Abbr.
9 Guinness superlative
10 "La ___ du jeu" (1939 Renoir film)
11 Music featured in "A Clockwork Orange"
12 "___ tu"
13 Faulty: Prefix
18 One who's working out of pocket, informally?
19 "Elf" co-star, 2003
24 Co-creator of "The Flintstones"
25 Curse
26 Memorable 2011 hurricane
27 Sights at Occupy protests
30 More
32 Stores
33 "Pagliacci" clown
34 Turns
36 Mushroom stem
38 ___ jolie
39 Chicago's Saint ___ University
44 Fishermen with traps
45 Browning piece
48 Hindu princess
50 Bad demonstrations
51 Prefix with -meter
52 Time out?
54 ___ fruit
56 On one's ___
57 When doubled, Miss Piggy's white poodle
58 N.H.L.'s Laperriere
59 Start of an alphabet book

by Stu Ockman

43 Medium

ACROSS
1 Flimflam
6 Char, as a steak
10 Handy roll-outs at sleepovers
14 ___ on (sentence shortener)
15 SeaWorld performer
16 Some
17 Throat lozenge for low-voiced opera stars?
19 See 43-Across
20 Museum piece
21 Certain weasel
22 Course with many unknowns: Abbr.
25 Cause of a sexual harassment complaint?
28 Dorm-mates, e.g.
30 Social finale?
31 Way to go: Abbr.
32 Its logo includes its name in blue letters in a yellow oval
33 Is miserly
35 Talk about pitchers and quarterbacks?
41 Pullman features
42 Class with a skeleton in the closet?: Abbr.
43 The Cavaliers of the 19-Across
45 Mate's approval
46 "Far out!"
49 Pub with no karaoke?
52 Kitchen meas.
53 Grad students' grillings
54 Dodges, perhaps
56 Woodsy scent
57 Admission provider for a kissing booth?
62 Flair
63 1968 winner of the 43-Down
64 Give birth, as a whale
65 Eliot who pursued Capone
66 Top dog
67 Home of Middle East University

DOWN
1 Terrif
2 Coded material
3 Some Super Bowl highlights
4 Red state, once
5 "The Sound of Music" tune
6 Some foods for growing babies
7 Hill of NBC News
8 Crackerjack pilot
9 U.K. military arm
10 Main section of a long poem
11 "No way!"
12 Precursor to a memorable Boston party
13 Wrap in bandages
18 Nobelist Wiesel
21 Exec's note taker
22 Lifeless
23 Crafty Norse god
24 Loses it
26 Foes of the Jedi
27 Commotion
29 Ceremonial rod
33 Urban grid: Abbr.
34 Start of a Clement Moore classic
36 Range extending from the Arctic to Kazakhstan
37 Eye annoyance
38 "___ the Boss" (Mick Jagger album)
39 Crashes into
40 Fred Astaire move
43 Annual tournament played in N.Y.C.
44 Manly
46 Mistreated
47 James with an electrical unit named after him
48 Beethoven's Third, popularly
50 Valleys
51 One of the Obamas
55 Con game
57 Cantankerous cry
58 "What's the ___?"
59 Alphabetic trio for fliers
60 Powerful Perón
61 Sum of the first three prime numbers

by Lynn Lempel

ACROSS

1 What ":" means on some exams
5 River in W.W. I fighting
9 Brewing giant
14 Kind of street
15 Top
16 Gray ones can cause arguments
17 *Look for
19 Caffè ___
20 "If only"
21 *Entice with
23 With 26-Across, none
24 Stumble
26 See 23-Across
27 Some investments, for short
28 *Drop one, say
31 Broker's goal
32 "Cold Mountain" novelist Charles
33 Most common first name among U.S. presidents (six)
34 *July, for Major League Baseball
37 Where lines may cross
40 Voluntarily, perhaps
43 Those Spaniards
44 *Doesn't worry
46 TV's onetime ___ Club
47 Electric ___
48 NetZero, e.g., for short
49 Zip

51 *It may bear a coat of arms
54 Relatives of raspberries
56 Succeed
57 *View from Land's End
59 Order countermanded by "Down, boy!"
60 Long haul
61 Legion
62 Travels over what's moving through the answers to the seven starred clues
63 Average
64 Bygone fliers

DOWN

1 "___ his kiss" (repeated 1964 lyric)
2 Suckler of Romulus and Remus
3 Sellout
4 What we share
5 Derisive call
6 See 13-Down
7 Exotic avian pets
8 Join forces anew
9 Tight
10 Man from Oman
11 Sony recorder
12 Twiddled one's thumbs
13 6-Down in sub-Saharan Africa

18 Salty orange square
22 Suffix with hex-
25 Stir at a speakeasy
29 Island birthplace of Epicurus
30 Spartan king who fought Pyrrhus
31 After-dinner drink, maybe
33 Holy Roman emperor during the War of the Spanish Succession
35 They include Cuba and Jamaica
36 Smart answers
37 Lower
38 It's south of Helsinki
39 Government study, briefly?
41 Spanish husbands
42 Ophthalmologist's procedure
44 Musical notes
45 Puts in, in a way
47 Fe, Ag, Au, etc.
50 Jrs. take them
52 "The Land of Painted Caves" novelist
53 Designed for flight
55 Singer Phil
58 End of a match, for short

by Kevin G. Der

45 MEDIUM

ACROSS

1 They may be kept on you
5 Massenet opera
10 Memo subject header
14 Stationery shade
15 "Care to?"
16 "Way cool!"
17 Capping
18 Herr Schindler with a list
19 Start of some carrier names
20 Manufacturers
22 Dangerous place
24 Tide competitor
25 "Apollo and Daphne" sculptor
26 ___ Marino
28 Three-way joint
30 Research aids
33 Beehive State player
34 Was out
37 Choir accompaniment
38 ___ fides (bad faith)
40 ___ water
42 Mother of Apollo
43 Chariot race site
45 One of the Munsters
47 Gen ___
48 Study of government
50 New England's Cape ___
51 Poetic preposition
52 Place to see a flick?
55 Bruins legend
57 Kind of well
59 Mythological figure being kissed in a statue at the Louvre
62 Old geezer
63 Spark producer
65 Parliament
66 Suffix in many store names
67 Botanist's concern
68 Salinger title girl
69 Scottish Gaelic
70 Aligns, briefly
71 Gym count

DOWN

1 ___ U.S.A.
2 ___ fool (be silly)
3 Possible reason for [see shaded letters]
4 Apartment 1A resident, perhaps
5 Infrequently seen bills
6 Suffers from
7 Place for an electronic tether
8 Where there are "bombs bursting," to an anthem singer
9 Polynesian wrap
10 All tangled up
11 Possible reason for [see shaded letters]
12 Like a blue lobster
13 School attended by King's Scholars
21 "Peanuts" expletive
23 Robert De ___
25 Geoffrey of fashion
26 "Poison" shrub
27 Producer of the 2600 game console
29 Musician/record producer Bobby
31 Stereotypical K.P. item
32 [So boring!]
35 High degree
36 "Hurry up!"
39 Liqueur served with coffee beans
41 Pewter component
44 Essen expletives
46 Son of Seth
49 Leaves a 0% tip
53 Ninth-inning excitement, maybe
54 OH− or Cl−, chemically
56 Truck rental company
57 Climber's goal
58 Zoo sound
59 H.S. supporters
60 Rope material
61 Verb with "vous"
64 Reactor-overseeing org.

by Peter A. Collins

ACROSS

1 Goof
7 Boo-boo
12 Player of TV's Caine
13 Circus performance or concert
16 Lined, as a furnace hearth
17 Representative's work
18 Nice one
19 L.A.P.D. part
20 Bro's greeting
21 With 29-/30-Across, wiggle room . . . or a hint to this puzzle's theme
23 "You ___!"
24 Stir
25 Monty Python title character
26 Chocolate dessert
28 It may have bullets
29 & 30 See 21-Across
33 Yuma-to-Tombstone dir.
34 Excuse
35 It may come from a well
36 Stumble, in a way
38 Kind of net
40 Ones stuck in the hospital, for short?
41 Approval in Rome
42 Medicine

44 Blue-roofed dining spots
45 "I heard ___!"
48 Shut-___
49 "Hold on"
50 Flushes
52 Quad bike, e.g.
53 2011 Rose Bowl winner, for short
54 One caught by border patrol
55 Market town that's a suburb of London
57 Folded like a fan
58 Mint
59 Gaffe
60 Screwup

DOWN

1 Film planner
2 Slugabed
3 First subway line in N.Y.C.
4 Grab a parking spot
5 Hit with, as a pickup line
6 Jet engine housings
7 Imperfect
8 Implements for "writing" on computer screens
9 Part of the face whose name is derived from the Latin for "grape"

10 1960s sitcom title character
11 Tubby
14 Gunk
15 Misprint
16 Flub
22 Old gang weapon
23 Prickly seedcase
26 Vocabulaire part
27 Get to
29 Rant
31 School whose football stadium is nicknamed the Horseshoe
32 Obeyer, as of laws
34 "You ___ me"
35 Brown, e.g.
37 Muff
39 Like New York's Waldorf-Astoria Hotel
40 Wallet items, in brief
41 Lord Byron's "___ Walks in Beauty"
43 Playwright Eve
44 Seen
45 Pratfall
46 The pits
47 It's not scripted
49 New Mexico county
51 Susan of Broadway's "Beauty and the Beast"
52 Eyebrow shape
56 Miss at a hoedown

by Jim Page

ACROSS

1 Act greedy
5 Newsman Lou
10 Stand taken by a debater
14 Elton John/Tim Rice musical
15 ___ Gay
16 Austen heroine
17 Jeering from the bleachers
18 Broom made of twigs
19 Crazy sort
20 End of some medieval tournament action?
23 Charger
26 Part of the translation of "anno Domini"
27 Weapons that hit in a medieval tournament?
33 Sum up
34 Holy book
35 Middleton and Moss
38 Estuaries
40 Track figure
42 Flood survivor
43 "The Most Happy ___"
45 Imitated a wolf
47 Spanish bear
48 Really boring medieval tournaments?
51 Actress Zadora
52 Unwelcome growth
53 Joking around at a medieval tournament?
60 See 58-Down
61 Noted declarer of bankruptcy in 2001
62 Olympics jump
66 W.W. II battle site
67 Accustom
68 "The occupation of the idle man, the distraction of the warrior, the peril of the sovereign," per Napoleon
69 Creature known scientifically as Bufo bufo
70 Heavy reading
71 Donald and Ivana, for instance

DOWN

1 Shoot the breeze
2 Carnival city
3 Fracas
4 Hamper
5 Actress Mazar
6 Fairly uncommon blood type, informally
7 Nonsense
8 Black mark
9 Biblical fellow who was dis-tressed?
10 "Back to the Future" transport
11 Mine, in Marseille
12 Springsteen's "___ Fire"
13 Told all to the cops
21 Mont. neighbor
22 Crud
23 Chow down on
24 ___ for (really delicious)
25 Ultimate object
28 Follower of many a dot
29 Some daily papers, informally
30 TV courtroom drama, 1986–94
31 Start or finish of an aphorism regarding justice
32 Patsy
36 Made less rigorous
37 Things binge drinkers sometimes do
39 Sloppy
41 Zebra
44 ___ were
46 Blue
49 Accept punishment
50 Entertain
53 Witticism
54 Anne Frank's father
55 Kareem Abdul-Jabbar's alma mater, in brief
56 ___ time at all
57 Oil container

by Karen Young Bonin

58 French artist famous for 60-Acrossing
59 Juana ___ de la Cruz, Mexican poet/nun
63 Losing row
64 Brink
65 French article

48 MEDIUM

ACROSS

1 Pass quickly, as on a highway
6 Rummage
10 Treat badly
14 Karma believer
15 Title accompanier: Abbr.
16 Team members
17 Many a nude beach visitor
18 ___ bread
19 Narc's find, perhaps
20 Subject with force
22 Perfectly behaved
24 Not under any circumstances
26 Big name in vacuums
27 Furnace fuel
31 Heals, in a way
33 Has a tab
34 The One, in "The Matrix"
35 Kind of pitcher
40 Storage unit
42 Maintains, as an itinerary
43 Double-check, e.g.
44 One of two in Monopoly
45 Port. is part of it
46 Word needed to be added to 12 appropriately placed answers in this puzzle for their clues to make sense

48 Music genre
49 Spills
53 Synonym source
55 Gives away, in a way
57 Braces
62 "___ la Douce"
63 14-Across V.I.P.
65 Back in
66 "The Big Lebowski" director
67 George Orwell's alma mater
68 Part of many a generator
69 Bandy, as ideas
70 Waste time
71 Act rowdily

DOWN

1 Get many price quotes
2 Drugged out
3 One's partner
4 Works of Horace
5 Famous cloth locale
6 List of criminals?
7 Magazine once published by Playboy
8 Senator's home
9 Comparison connector
10 Wild card
11 Banish
12 Vestige
13 Wander aimlessly

21 Less sophisticated, in a way
23 "Check it out!"
25 Exclamation of surprise
27 Change one's opinion
28 Meany of story
29 Items sometimes tossed in strongman contests
30 Biblical twin
32 Rancher, typically
36 Hosp. employees
37 Golfer Aoki
38 Cry of shocked hurt
39 Not be serious
41 Military leaders
42 Group leaders
44 The Smothers Brothers, e.g.
47 Showy
49 Linger
50 "Vive ___!"
51 Ancient Mexican
52 Party principle
54 Johnny Storm a k a the Human ___
56 City near Provo
58 But, in Bolivia
59 Standout
60 Still-life subjects
61 Search here and there
64 Digits, e.g.: Abbr.

by Jeff Chen

ACROSS

1 Noted handler of dogs
7 Mother of Helios
11 Tubes
14 Sports star who wrote 2009's "Open: An Autobiography"
15 Whom Othello declares "is most honest"
16 Actress Charlotte
17 Security desk at a Broadway theater?
19 ___ de France
20 Starts at either end?
21 Certain Alaskan
22 Large bra feature
23 Simian on a Broadway set?
26 Challenge for a H.S. honor student
29 Author Dinesen
30 "Even ___ speak . . ."
31 ___ & Young (accounting firm)
34 Cancel
37 Understudy in a Broadway show?
41 Place with a waiting room: Abbr.
42 Gather
43 Son or grandson, say
44 Italian beloved

46 Greek peak SE of Olympus
48 Pessimistic Broadway investors?
53 Owns, in the Bible
54 Actress Rene
55 "___ made clear . . ."
58 Egg: Prefix
59 Nighttime Broadway wardrobe?
62 "The Simpsons" character who says "Oh geez" a lot
63 [Giggle]
64 It's awesome
65 Mac alternatives
66 Love god
67 ___ régime (pre-1789 French government)

DOWN

1 Whittle (down)
2 A long, long time
3 Plumbers' wheels
4 D-Day craft, for short
5 Walt Disney had 26 of them
6 Color akin to plum
7 Emperor who completed the Colosseum
8 Author Bret
9 A star can have a huge one

10 CD mailer of the early 2000s
11 Bad conditions for playing hoops, say
12 Care about
13 Running slowly
18 "Sesame Street" supporter, in brief
22 Strands in a cell?
23 Will of "The Waltons"
24 Odds and ends: Abbr.
25 Bone: Prefix
26 Circus cries
27 Natl. Merit Scholarship qualifying exam
28 Minneapolis/St. Paul
31 Green org.
32 Literary inits.
33 "Stillmatic" rapper
35 "Last one ___ a rotten egg!"
36 More, in adspeak
38 ___ avis
39 Slate, e.g.
40 Conductance units
45 Rhine whine?
46 Siege site of A.D. 72
47 ___ horse
48 Bite
49 Rack and ruin
50 Prefix with -pedic
51 M.T.A. fleet

by Kevan Choset

52 Subj. of a space-to-Earth experiment on Apollo 14

55 Mine, in Amiens

56 "Me, too"

57 Library ID

59 Tony-winning role for Mandy Patinkin

60 ___ Lingus

61 "Desperate Housewives" network

ACROSS

1 Add-on to the start or end of a word stem (as in 17-, 25-, 35-, 49- and 57-Across)
6 Forward
11 Players who spend most of their time on the bench, briefly
14 ___ Club, 1930s–60s New York hot spot
15 Peer of Ellington
16 Fish of the genus Moringua
17 Unnecessary words cluttering wise sayings?
19 Rai ___ (Italian TV channel)
20 Google results
21 Dropper?
22 See 36-Down
24 ___ Shuffle (boxing move)
25 Threat in "Armageddon"?
28 Salad bar tidbit
30 Pile of glacial debris
31 When repeated, words before "burning bright" to start a William Blake poem
32 Bark
34 Nap finish?

35 Good place for a picnic?
38 German interjections
41 Honor His Honor, say
42 Pushes for
46 Fly-catching birds
48 Out
49 Like a tenacious sibling?
52 Nutritional fig.
53 Additions and deletions, say
54 Soak
55 Old Dodge
56 Sharp-edged tool
57 "We've taken the city, but can we defend it"?
61 Festa de ___ João
62 Native parka wearer
63 Sharp-crested ridge
64 Directional ending
65 Peter who directed "The Dresser"
66 Like an unlucky encierro participant

DOWN

1 Urban playground surface
2 Kansas mil. post built in 1853
3 Support
4 Sportscaster Cross and others
5 Classic Jaguar
6 Arafat successor

7 Israel's third-largest city
8 That: Sp.
9 Insurance giant on the N.Y.S.E.
10 Further in
11 City named after the French for "strait"
12 Princess Leia, e.g.
13 Not Rubens's type
18 Agitate
23 They can be felt in a classroom
25 Extreme
26 Belted, in the Bible
27 It's sold in tubs
29 Least windy
32 Top of a bottom
33 Former intelligence agcy.
36 Three-term title for 22-Across: Abbr.
37 Like some lips
38 Quiet, in a way
39 Cheeseburger cheese
40 A ship may appear on it
43 More likely to make you sick, say
44 Postscript
45 Like some glass or wood
47 Europe's Bay of —
48 L'Eiger, e.g.
50 -like
51 Runaways
55 Spanish alternative?

by Steven E. Atwood

58 Brazilian greeting
59 Take home
60 Not stay all the
   way up

51 MEDIUM

ACROSS

1 Web programmer's medium
5 Telly network
8 Hunter who wrote "The Blackboard Jungle"
12 Grammy winner India.___
13 Glowing rings
15 Prop for Houdini
16 Subject for a Degas painting
18 Patron saint of Norway
19 Complete train wreck, in Southern slang
20 "Gimme ___!"
21 Bedsheets and such
24 Not in stock, but coming
26 Prize higher than plata or bronce
27 Stable father figure?
31 ___ lot (gorged oneself)
32 Software prototype
34 ___ bene
36 Has no stomach for
39 Classic Xavier Cugat song . . . or a hint to the invitation in the circled letters
42 Field on screen
43 R&B singer Peniston
44 Unaccompanied performances

45 Impart
47 Like some vowels and pants
49 "Platoon" setting, informally
50 Fast-food franchise with a game piece in its logo
53 Locales for crow's-nests
55 Those, to Teodoro
56 Parody singer Yankovic
60 Rebuke to a traitor
61 Snaking, like the arrangement of circled letters in this puzzle
65 Rudolph and kin
66 Paraffin-coated Dutch imports
67 Periodic table info: Abbr.
68 Dover delicacy
69 Prefix with functional
70 Host Mike of the Discovery Channel's "Dirty Jobs"

DOWN

1 Feasted on
2 "La-la" lead-in
3 Least fig.
4 Milk, to Manuel
5 Scottish slope
6 Banquo, in Verdi's "Macbeth"
7 Aircraft division of Textron

8 Green nuts?
9 Parking amenities
10 Tequila source
11 "In your dreams!"
13 Malfunction, with "up"
14 German city on the Danube
17 Time immemorial
21 University of New Mexico team
22 Grantorto's victim in "The Faerie Queene"
23 Secret rendezvous point
25 "The wearin' ___ green"
28 Queen of Thebes, in myth
29 Sgt.'s program
30 Bluesy Waters
33 Idle
35 "With the bow," to a violinist
37 Razzle-dazzle
38 Removes cream from
40 Vegas casino magnate Steve
41 Bard's nightfall
46 Used a divining rod
48 Gangbuster
50 Some Monopoly cards
51 Prefix with arthritis
52 Zero-star, say
54 Wedding day destination

by Elizabeth C. Gorski

57 Some investments, for short
58 45 letters
59 ___ Moines
62 "What am ___ do?"
63 San Antonio-to-Amarillo dir.
64 Abbr. in a job ad

ACROSS

1 Org. whose annual budget is classified information
4 Establishes
11 Part of T.G.I.F.
14 Parrot
15 Pottery whose high iron content gives it a distinctive hue
16 Cry heard at Moe's bar
17 "Hee Haw," for one
19 Lennon reportedly described her as looking like "a bloke in drag"
20 Attended to pressing matters?
21 Thought
23 Classroom array
24 Noted Irish crystal
26 "___ does not surpass nature, but only brings it to perfection": Cervantes
27 Hägar's daughter in the comics
28 Looking up
29 Mass exodus of a sort
32 Air safety org.
34 Moral lapse that is reflected literally by the answers at 17-, 24-, 46- and 54-Across
38 Cabinet dept.

39 Wife of Orpheus
41 One in a prompt box
44 "Hey . . . over here!"
45 Capital of Australia: Abbr.
46 Physician with a D.O. degree
49 Come from behind
51 Mason's creator
52 Targets of some animal rights activists
53 Supermarket inits.
54 "When a Man Loves a Woman" singer
57 Pal of Marshall, Lily, Robin and Barney on "How I Met Your Mother"
58 "Got one's money's worth" at the smorgasbord
59 One-eighty
60 Sugar suffix
61 Tiresome
62 Old IBM products

DOWN

1 "Feliz ___"
2 Rack unit
3 Ford's first minivan
4 Ontario natives
5 Like the SST fleet: Abbr.
6 Big name in the freezer aisle
7 Reactions to puppies

8 Faa'a International Airport location
9 Undermine
10 "Ratatouille" setting
11 "Likewise"
12 Laser printer supplies
13 Poorly made
18 Sign
22 Lily-livered
24 Threadbare
25 One of four in " 'Twas the night before Christmas, when all through the house"
27 Earth mover
30 Rode a thermal current
31 U.P.S. delivery: Abbr.
32 Old fur trader's locale
33 Actress Adams
35 Thrill
36 Approached furtively
37 Environment-related
40 Champs-___
41 Start of a line ending in a sum?
42 Linguists' concerns
43 Brokerage firm with talking baby ads
44 Got a 3 on the 17th at Sawgrass, e.g.
47 Doped up, in a way

by Bill Thompson

48 Pet ____
49 Cameos, e.g.
50 "Fables in Slang" humorist George

52 Queue after Q
55 Dernier ____
56 Ming of the N.B.A.

ACROSS

1 Hit 1942 film with the song "Love Is a Song"
6 Pack (down)
10 Maybe too smooth
14 Starter of a 58-Down
15 Many a cut, eventually
16 Page, e.g.
17 Dagger's partner
18 Like some sloths
20 Legal deadlock
22 Relatives of aardwolves
23 Pollution watchdog org.
24 Bank list
25 Bookie's concern
30 Pink-slip
33 Carnival attractions
34 Dissolve with acid, say
35 Acid neutralizer
36 War, famine, etc.
37 They're crossed by bridges
39 Give a thumbs-up on Facebook
40 Nappers catch them
41 Bobby of the rink
42 Shaved
43 Goof
44 Most stand-up comedy acts
47 Stroked
48 Farm abode
49 Sagittarius, with "the"
52 Bush cabinet member
57 1863 speech opener
59 Do like some birds and bees
60 90° from norte
61 Mop, say
62 Confederate
63 Do some gardening
64 Trick-taking card game
65 Mid-March celebration . . . or a hint to the starts of 18-, 25-, 44- and 57-Across

DOWN

1 "Brandenburg Concertos" composer
2 Censorship-fighting org.
3 Natural satellite
4 Egotist's comment
5 Some printers
6 Feature of some high heels
7 Hurting
8 Disrupt, say
9 Gets ready, as an oven
10 Bush cabinet member
11 Symbol on Sri Lanka's flag
12 Word exclaimed after "no" or "good"
13 Hospital capacity
19 Inspected
21 DHL competitor
24 Guinness Book entry
25 Cherish
26 Titan, once
27 Loiterer
28 Lake of cryptozoological interest
29 Violate a peace treaty, maybe
30 Tahrir Square's locale
31 Catawampus
32 Budget priorities
35 Snooze-inducing
37 Kansas City ___, Negro Leagues team with Satchel Paige, Jackie Robinson and Ernie Banks
38 Utah city
42 Get pumped
44 Is in the hole
45 Declare
46 Highest degree
47 Bit of evidence
49 More than one
50 Levitated
51 Buttonlike?
52 "Nessun dorma," for one
53 Pasta, in product names
54 He wrote "Jupiter from on high laughs at lovers' perjuries"

by Dave Sarpola

55 Greek cheese
56 Long shot,
in hoops
58 See 14-Across

54 MEDIUM

ACROSS

1 Language in which "hello" is "kaixo"
7 Chop-chop
11 Consumer protection org.
14 "Phooey!"
15 Hit song with the line "When she squeezed me tight she nearly broke my spine"
16 French word that sounds like a letter of the alphabet
17 Rows
18 Grin-and-bear-it types
20 Impatient leprechaun's concern on an airplane?
22 Gossip
25 Type
26 Modernists
27 Musical genre of Jimmy Eat World
28 Southern Iraqi city
30 Ooze
31 Degree for a leprechaun who's an expert at finding imperfections?
34 Period when Long Island was formed
35 Some electronic parts
39 Leprechaun's book detailing the truth about flounders?

43 Basic point
45 Show biz elite
46 Chess pieces
47 "The Long, Hot Summer" woman ___ Varner
48 Mussorgsky's "Pictures ___ Exhibition"
49 New York's ___ River
50 Scary legislation introduced by a leprechaun?
54 Rare astronomical event
55 Maharishi, e.g.
59 Score keeper, for short?
60 Obama education secretary Duncan
61 Part of the Iroquois Confederacy
62 Nice 'n Easy product
63 1987 Costner role
64 Vamp

DOWN

1 Punch accompanier
2 Knock over
3 Kind of short
4 Fantasy novel element
5 Miners' sch.
6 Latin 101 verb
7 Swiss city where William Tell shot an apple

8 Sisterly
9 Up
10 Beatle who was born with the first name James
11 Any of the singers of "Jive Talkin'"
12 Paint the town red, maybe
13 Goes over 21 at the casino
19 Clorox cleaner
21 Brand name in a blue oval
22 Brat Packer Moore
23 Apple choice
24 Symbol of the Virgin Mary
28 Fathered
29 Aphrodite's lover
30 Fleet
32 Home-shopping event?
33 Troubles
36 Russian diet
37 Squeezes (out)
38 Text message status
40 Sugar daddies, e.g.
41 Bygone Manhattan eatery
42 TV journalist Lisa
43 Word from a foreman
44 Unjust treatment
47 Died down
48 Previously, to poets
49 County on the Thames

by Kristian House

51 Arab nation that's
   not in OPEC
52 Insurance grps.
53 Newcastle's river

56 Good thing that comes
   to those who wait?
57 Formal "yes"
58 Hipster

55 MEDIUM

ACROSS

1 Says impulsively
7 Everything
13 Southwestern spread
14 Precious
15 Harm
16 Horsehide leather
17 Men's patriotic org.
18 Lower
20 Evening on the Arno
21 Walt Frazier or Patrick Ewing
23 Some museum pieces
25 Over there
26 Danish shoe company
27 Fraternity letters
28 Horseshoe-shaped fastener
30 Nickname for 42-Across
33 Bummed
34 The U.K. is in it, but Ire. is not
35 Rainy and cold
36 Exit key
37 Willing
39 Day-___
42 Singer born March 25, 1942
46 Mural painter Rivera
47 Koh-i-___ diamond
48 Fill
49 Where IVs might be hooked up
50 ___ Penh

52 ___ Bees (big company in personal care products)
53 A ponytail hangs over it
55 "Yowzer!"
57 Biblical judge
58 Holders of frozen assets?
60 Withstood
62 Religious figures
63 Specifically
64 Largest city on the Belgian coast
65 Examined thoroughly, with "through"

DOWN

1 Meat cuts
2 Sancho Panza's land
3 Yet to be tagged, say
4 Elvis's label
5 1968 hit for 42-Across
6 Irked
7 ___ Haute
8 "I've ___ it!"
9 God whose name is 6-Down reversed
10 See 52-Down
11 Putting up big numbers
12 Studio occupant, e.g.
14 Recess rebuttal, perhaps

16 1967 hit for 42-Across
19 Family room fixture
22 ___ au vin
24 "Valley of the Dolls" author
27 It has fuzz
29 End of many a concert
31 Pull a cork out of
32 Brother
36 Mental image, for short?
38 Bouquet
39 Gave the evil eye
40 1962 Neil Simon musical
41 Not bilateral
42 Chuck Yeager and others
43 1967 hit for 42-Across
44 Irks
45 The Wildcats of the Big 12 Conf.
46 Bickle portrayer in "Taxi Driver"
51 Stash
52 With 10-Down, 1967 hit for 42-Across
54 Suffix with kitchen
56 Bell ___
59 Howard of Hollywood
61 Like Beethoven's Sixth Symphony

1	2	3	4	5	6	████	████	7	8	9	10	11	12
13						████	14						
15						████	16						
17			████	18		19			████	20			
21			22		████	23			24	████	25		
26				████	27			████	28	29			
30			31				32						████
33			████	34			████	35			████	████	████
████	████	████	36			████	37	38			████	39	40	41
████	42	43			44				45			
46				████	47				████	48			
49			████	50	51			████	52			
53			54	████	55			56	████	57		
58				59			████	60		61		
62						████	63					
64						████	65					

by Peter A. Collins and Joe Krozel

56 MEDIUM

ACROSS

1 The Rhinemaidens in the "Ring" cycle, e.g.
8 Cracks up
15 Hot stuff
16 Went for on a gut feeling
17 Wing part
18 Their images are out of this world
19 Entrees for one of Dion's backup singers?
21 Ballpark figs.
22 "Who's there?" reply
23 Weapon in some raids
26 W.W. II arena
27 Late-night TBS show
29 Old royal
30 Discounts at garages?
34 Luau side dish
35 Singer
36 Severely reduced wagers?
43 Circus sounds
44 ". . . ___ wed"
45 Like a line whose slope is zero: Abbr.
48 Sweetheart
49 Forum garb
51 ___ Valley
52 What mechanics may do as part of a tuneup?
56 Irish lass

58 Ones requesting seconds?
59 Primed
60 Not so fast
61 Showed reverence for, in a way
62 Orbital figure

DOWN

1 One making camp?
2 White-collar worker
3 Antique desk feature
4 Celebrity couples, usually
5 Rookie: Var.
6 Big campaign topic: Abbr.
7 "Great" part for Duvall
8 Danger for wearers of high-heel shoes
9 O. Henry Award winner for "In the Region of Ice" (1967) and "The Dead" (1973)
10 China's Zhou ___
11 Valentine letters?
12 Wearer of a crown since 1952
13 Absorbed the cost of
14 Some A.L. batters
20 "South Park" boy
24 Ringo's drumming son

25 Grp. with a complex code
27 Shorten
28 1930s migrant
29 Casse-___ (French brainteaser)
31 Many downloads
32 "Bramble ___" (book of Robert Bridges poems)
33 Casino collector
36 Certain tooth
37 Flat-headed tool
38 Current principle
39 Start chowing down
40 Opposite of legato: Abbr.
41 U2 member
42 Disturb
46 Met expectations?
47 Brawl in the backwoods
49 In a tough spot
50 Plain
51 Silents star Nita
53 Palindromic magazine title
54 Small knot
55 Very, informally
56 Ear piece?
57 Celebrity widowed in 1980

by Alan Arbesfeld

ACROSS

1 Barbers' aids
6 Like some batters
10 Hurry it up
14 Available for mugs
15 Added, in commercialese
16 Pizarro foe
17 Flirty one
18 Man's labor?
20 Christina of "Sleepy Hollow"
22 Barbecue grill brand
23 Woman's flippant remark?
28 Wrangler rival
29 "___ Miss Brooks"
30 Golden, in México
31 Not stay rigid
32 Sweet-talk
35 Garden decoration
37 Woman's journalism?
43 NutraSweet rival
44 "___ Hall"
45 Spiral shape
48 Branches of study
51 "Is there something more?"
52 Lob's path
53 Woman's package?
56 You're being attacked while under it
58 "Vive ___!"
59 Man's plank?
63 Magazine revenue source
66 Sea lettuce, e.g.
67 Something many a celebrity carries in public
68 Towering
69 Pay attention to
70 Skirmish
71 Utah's ___ Canyon

DOWN

1 Foldout bed
2 Telephone key with no letters
3 Highest peak in Turk.
4 Nuts-and-bolts
5 Tiny bit
6 Splitsville resident?
7 Bygone muscle car
8 [Damn, this is frustrating!]
9 Talk and talk
10 In great supply
11 Powerless
12 Lint catcher
13 Enmity
19 Have
21 Fish salted for bacalao
23 Andean stimulant
24 River to the Rhine
25 Iditarod transport
26 River near the Leaning Tower
27 Sound from a pound
31 Conk
33 Cambodian money
34 1974 John Wayne film
36 Advanced deg. for musicians
38 Bash on a beach
39 Make
40 Right away
41 One of the Flying Wallendas
42 Actress Lamarr
45 The Clash's "Rock the ___"
46 American Leaguer since 1954
47 When mastodons became extinct
49 Like some amusement park passes
50 "Told ya!"
53 Crash site?
54 Floss brand
55 Big name in travel guides
57 Sheepskin holder
60 Dolt
61 Warm lining
62 Laundry day brand
64 And the like: Abbr.
65 Look over

by Joe DiPietro

ACROSS

1 Cigar's end?
5 Some CD players
8 Source of Erebus and Gaia, in Greek myth
13 What a welcome sight relieves
15 Spring locale
16 Words sung to the beginning of 41-/39-Across
18 Handle orders (for), briefly
19 Community near Los Angeles
20 Carry-___
21 Carry-___
22 Smoothness
27 Judge
29 Carrier whose main hub is Kastrup airport
31 ___ alla genovese
32 Two-time opponent of 69-Down
34 Middle of the title of many an ode
36 Copy cats?
37 Often-chanted letters
39 See 41-Across
41 With 39-Across, a familiar tune
45 D.D.E.'s veep
46 On a streak?
47 Sink
49 Cousin of a bittern
53 Exhaust

55 CD follower
57 Ballesteros of golf
58 Designated
60 Place for a butcher and two others
62 Food container
63 English complexion
65 "Do continue . . ."
66 Words sung to the beginning of 41-/39-Across
71 Stirred
72 Part of a duelist's uniform
73 Run
74 Tulsa sch.
75 Capital of Chile

DOWN

1 "CHiPs" co-star, 1977–83
2 Dried (off)
3 Still life feature?
4 Bard's dusk
5 "Bob ___ Greatest Hits" (1967 top 10 album)
6 Makes fun of
7 Former fliers
8 Like some washers or arcade games
9 Solo in space
10 "Shoot!"
11 Monet medium
12 Beijing-to-Shanghai dir.

14 Big name in kitchenware
17 Doo-___
23 Mindless followers
24 Rhône feeder
25 Shop
26 Greeting that might be made with a tip of the hat
28 Resting place
30 Resting place
33 Puerto Rico, e.g.
35 Come from ___
38 "Woe is me!"
40 Handy sort?
41 It can be dunked
42 Soak
43 Electrician's alloy
44 Kind of power
48 Commence hostilities
50 Push back further
51 Demonstrates
52 Takes care of
54 Ate like a bird
56 Waikiki wear
59 Slip on
61 ___ Mawr
64 An apple with a bite out of it, for one
66 Nail
67 Pooh pal
68 Blue state?
69 Two-time opponent of 32-Across
70 Org. for Agassi

by Milo Beckman

ACROSS

1 Frankenstein's monster had one on his forehead
5 Crop circle, some believe
9 Mahmoud of the P.L.O.
14 Lasso
15 ___ child
16 Word sung twice before "hallelujah"
17 One who's junior to a jr.
18 Acts the heckler at the Westminster dog show?
20 Commemorative item
22 Busy one
23 "Scat!"
24 Cheeses manufactured in the Mediterranean?
26 D flat equivalent
28 Cousin of .org or .com
29 ___ standstill
30 Baseball Hall-of-Famer who batted left and threw right
31 Stack in a mag. office
32 Pondered
34 Furbys and yo-yos, once
37 Entourages for Odysseus' faithful wife?
41 Lorna ___ (cookies)

42 Jot (down)
44 "___ Chef"
47 Amusement
48 Long time
50 Blast
51 Quick smells
53 Ricky Martin and Neil Patrick Harris?
55 "___ dead people"
56 Cousin of an ostrich
58 Department in SE France
59 Expressions of regret from apartment building managers?
62 Icelandic epic
64 Skipping syllables
65 Romance/thriller novelist Hoag
66 McDonald's founder Ray
67 Intelligence
68 1982 sci-fi film with a 2010 sequel
69 Harmonize, informally

DOWN

1 Class of '12 in 2012, e.g.: Abbr.
2 Confined
3 Flashing sign in a TV studio
4 What a user goes into for help
5 "Que sera sera"
6 Odysseus' savior

7 Lumps
8 It lists G.M. and I.B.M.
9 Long ___
10 Bit of makeup
11 John of Led Zeppelin
12 Enthusiasms
13 Online network admins
19 Not just busy
21 Giving up of one thing for another
24 Half a school yr.
25 Irish equivalent of Edward
27 Source of the all-time best-selling movie-related toy line
30 Quick round of tennis
33 Cut off
35 Copy
36 Special delivery?: Abbr.
38 No-goodniks
39 Spelling, e.g.?
40 Continued, as with a job
43 Some records, for short
44 Features of many spy films
45 "I bet!"
46 Tin tossed as the first Frisbee
49 Sun-Maid tidbit

by Zoe Wheeler

52 Intuits
53 Dearie
54 Less-than-social sorts
57 Politico Romney
60 Singer Corinne Bailey ___
61 Med. group
63 Va. Tech is in it

Note: When this crossword is done, the puzzle's theme will help you fill the interior squares.

ACROSS

1 Group of mountains
7 ___ a one
11 Perk for a C.E.O., maybe
14 1992 Wimbledon winner
15 Comics character who almost never speaks
16 Cry spelled with an accent on the last letter
17 Pastime for Napoleon and Fidel Castro
19 Tube top
20 Oarlock
21 ___ terrier
22 E-help page
25 It prompted a flood of "Psycho" analysis
27 Bank of Israel
29 Woody part of Ohio?
30 Songlike
31 Understands, to a Scot
32 One way to choose
33 Stop on ___
36 "Lou Grant" paper, with "the"
37 Where King Arthur was conveyed for his wounds to be healed
38 Make part of the mix
42 Stanley who wrote "George Mills"
43 Chosen beforehand

47 Org. in '70s headlines
48 ___ Hashana
49 Long-___
50 Prefix with posit
51 Things waved at the Indy 500
57 Photog's master
58 Spanish direction
59 Cologne brand
60 Govt.-issued ID
61 Come clean, with "up"
62 Bomb defusers, often

DOWN

1 16 or Seventeen, for short
2 Turkish title
3 Tom Hanks's "Sleepless in Seattle" role
4 Vancouver-to-Seattle dir.
5 Uniform: Prefix
6 Bottle of whiskey
7 Not in any way, informally
8 Title role in a 1975 Truffaut film
9 Choir's platform
10 "I'll do it!"
11 Colorful riding gear
12 Funny Boosler
13 Cones on plains
18 One-third of Neapolitan, for short

21 Prelude to a resignation, perhaps
22 Liposuction target
23 Eagle's nest: Var.
24 Bee production
25 ___ Chapel
26 Collected, as wheat
28 Like Shakespeare's Othello
34 Work hard
35 Sicilian province or its capital
38 Blacksmiths' wear
39 Crowds
40 Does something about something
41 Square at the end of the fourth row in Battleship
44 It has terms regarding a term
45 Breaks down
46 Whodunit award
51 Make some calls
52 Big do, for short
53 Testing zone
54 Te ___
55 "Go on now!"
56 Grilling sound

by Elizabeth C. Gorski

ACROSS

1 From now on
6 Brewery supply
10 Pound sterling
14 Honolulu's ___ Tower
15 Inner: Prefix
16 "Go back," on an edit menu
17 Strike
20 Suffix with symptom
21 Rangers, on a sports ticker
22 "Save Me" singer Mann
23 Search for
25 Memo abbr.
27 Strike
32 Braid
35 Airs now
36 Lobster eater's wear
37 Carnival follower
38 Famed batter in an 1888 poem
40 Sometimes-saturated substances
41 Lansing-to-Flint dir.
42 Seldom seen
43 Try to corner the market on
44 Strike
48 Dairy section selection
49 Take a good look at
53 Bit of wisdom
56 Slow-pitch path
57 Rich soil
58 Result of three strikes for 38-Across
62 Patron saint of Norway
63 Bucks' mates
64 Printing press part
65 Feudal worker
66 River through Florence
67 Like dorm rooms, often

DOWN

1 Radical Mideast group
2 Best of the best
3 "And that's the truth!"
4 Women's fiction, slangily
5 Use knife and fork, say
6 Regarding this point
7 Jet-black gem
8 School grp.
9 "Help!" at sea
10 Like many shops at Disneyland
11 One in a mint?
12 Not active
13 Lavish affection (on)
18 ". . . three men in ___"
19 Squelched
24 ___ Chex
25 Religious mosaic locale
26 Where Paris took Helen
28 Gets up
29 Cyberspace marketplace
30 In ___ (as found)
31 Dosage amt.
32 Commoner
33 TV host with a college degree in speech therapy
34 From the top
38 Punish, in a way
39 Golden Fleece ship
40 Gas tank-to-engine connector
42 N.B.A. coach Pat
43 Item with straps
45 Leave a Web page, perhaps
46 David of "CSI: Miami"
47 One way to store data
50 Whites' counterparts
51 Big name in jewelry
52 Tip reducer?
53 Calendario units
54 McCain : 2008 :: ___ : 1996
55 Nearly shut
56 Service closer
59 Muckraker Tarbell
60 And not
61 Energy

by David Kwong

ACROSS

1 Govt. org. whose logo depicts an eagle standing on a key
4 Actress Veronica who was the model in the last cigarette ad shown on U.S. TV
9 Backyard event, informally
14 View from Casablanca: Abbr.
15 Item on a toothpick, maybe
16 Stop abruptly
17 I.S.P. giant
18 Queen of India
19 Persian Gulf port
20 Founder of the 26-/21-Down
23 Initial feeling?
24 It helps you get a handle on things
25 It's a thought
27 Torch bearer
28 Norma of "Sunset Boulevard"
32 White jacket, often
35 Core
36 Computer maker
37 Unimagined
38 Clearance sites?
42 Vocabulary-related
45 Kind of wave
46 Judiciary checker: Abbr.
47 Forage storage

48 Faucet attachment
52 Steamy place
55 Some 26-/21-Down volunteers
57 Capital of the country that's alphabetically first in the United Nations
59 Some Beethoven works
60 The Battle Born State: Abbr.
61 "Go farther" sloganeer, once
62 Lassitude
63 Break
64 Debussy contemporary
65 Breaks
66 Lack of focus, colloquially

DOWN

1 Annual Image Awards grp.
2 Alternative to Putinka, briefly
3 Literary middle name
4 He is "more an antique Roman than a Dane," in literature
5 Georgia's on its side
6 Where long-distance calls are made in the Mideast?
7 ___ since
8 It flows with the wind

9 Cool quality, in modern slang
10 "Father of," in Arabic
11 "Judge Judy" coverage?
12 Victoria's Secret merchandise
13 Medicine applicator
21 See 26-Down
22 Poetry volume
26 With 21-Down, humanitarian organization
29 10 sawbucks
30 ESPN ticker abbr.
31 Computer maker
32 Workout target, for short
33 Yearn
34 When doubled, a vitamin deficiency
39 1929 #1 hit whose title follows the line "Now he's gone and we're through"
40 Cultivate
41 Transport on two wheels
42 Openings
43 Deleted, as text
44 Abnormal dryness, to a dermatologist
49 Fiji's neighbor to the east
50 Mountain nymph
51 Answered

by Michael Shteyman

52 They're lifted on chairlifts

53 "No ___ nada" ("Don't worry about it": Sp.)

54 Neighbor

56 Department of NW France

58 Israeli weapon

ACROSS

1 Brubeck of jazz
5 Newscaster Connie
10 Gumbo need
14 iPad owner's subscription
15 Hes
16 Take seriously
17 Canine on a feline
18 Get the better of
19 Victim of Pizarro
20 Makes a father of
22 As well
24 Growls like a dog
25 Have a loan from
27 Actress Scala
29 Pitcher Maglie who was outdueled in Don Larsen's 1956 perfect game
30 Forearm bone-related
32 Five Norse kings
34 Kind of dye
35 "___ Fuehrer's Face"
37 ___ nitrite (angina treatment)
38 Hoedown activity . . . or what each group of circled letters is?
41 Steady guy
43 Carnaby Street type of the '60s
44 Saldana of "Avatar"
45 Rash-causing shrub
47 Gaynor of "South Pacific"
49 CBS series set in Vegas
52 Constellation with the Stingray Nebula
53 Microwave brand
55 Place to dry out
57 Margin in a baseball squeaker
59 Japanese flower-arranging art
61 Declines, with "out"
62 Sir or madam
64 ___ Ishii ("Kill Bill" character)
65 Hostess snack cake
66 S.U.V. named for a lake
67 Leave in the dust
68 Places for baths
69 Traffic problem
70 Hit 1998 animated movie

DOWN

1 Clears, as a windshield
2 Cuneiform discovery site
3 Graffiti artist, perhaps
4 See 38-Down
5 "Let's go!"
6 Boy band with the hit "MMMBop"
7 Suffix with glob
8 Fixed by a vet
9 Subject of a 1982 best seller on sexuality
10 State with a large Amish population
11 Casino attraction with a "bubble"
12 Make right
13 Toothpaste letters
21 Onetime Trooper and Rodeo maker
23 "You suck!"
26 Attacked energetically
28 Words for the deaf: Abbr.
31 Rich soil
33 Spike, as punch
34 Pastel hue
36 Give a Bronx cheer
38 With 4-Down, "The Collector" co-star
39 Like surnames ending in -escu
40 Bête ___
41 "Be Prepared" org.
42 ABBA's music genre
46 Part of a Lionel set
48 Either of two characters in "The Emperor's New Clothes"
49 Styx ferryman
50 Least likely to lose it
51 Big guitar brand
54 Pups without papers
56 "The Hot Zone" virus
58 Those, in Tijuana
60 Boat's backbone
61 17 of them are sung before "my gosh" in a 2010 #1 Usher hit
63 Everyday article in rap titles

by Steven Riley

64 MEDIUM

ACROSS

1 It can change one's tune
5 Before the procedure, informally
10 Abbr. on many a cornerstone
14 ___ Trevelyan, villain in the James Bond film "GoldenEye"
15 Must
16 Wolf whistle accompanier, maybe
17 Put in the hole
18 Question asked in Matthew 26:22
19 Actress Steppat of "On Her Majesty's Secret Service"
20 World capital at 7,200+ feet elevation
22 Certain Ghostbuster
23 Groks
24 "Thank you," in Swahili
26 Carps
28 Blood feud
30 One of a pair of items often given at a baby shower
31 Stellar start?
32 "Das ___" (Volkswagen slogan)
34 Shows the door
35 Nonmembers . . . or what 4-, 7- and 10-Down lack?

38 Pharmacy stock
41 Part of a landscaping team
42 Makeover
46 Old Shaker leader
48 Like horseshoes on barn doors
50 Embarks
52 He once wrote "Last but not least, avoid clichés like the plague"
53 "Star Trek: T.N.G." role
54 Slant
56 Trig function
57 Blarney source
58 Following behind
60 Barbecue fare
61 It may be broken into on Broadway
62 Jean-Luc Godard film "___ Musique"
63 Spymaster's worry
64 Put in a difficult spot
65 Music's Stefani and others
66 Recording artist made famous by the BBC series "The Celts"

DOWN

1 Tapioca source
2 Ellery Queen and others
3 It's decided in the fall
4 Checker or Domino
5 Fraternity character
6 Destroy, in Devon

7 It may include two weeks' notice
8 10th-century Holy Roman emperor
9 End of many trips
10 John Calvin, e.g.
11 Superior things
12 Drug or DNA home-use set
13 Does a morning routine
21 Corroded
25 Floride, par exemple
27 Ones protected by a safety net, with "the"
29 Bottom
33 Ancient concert halls
36 Gets high, say
37 Dwarf planet beyond Pluto
38 Most widespread
39 Mistakenly
40 Fats Domino's real first name
43 Dictionary specification
44 So as to last
45 It's far from shore
47 Providing relief for
49 ___ Neuchâtel
51 "You don't have to tell me"
55 Old-looking
59 Montgomery of jazz

by Sean Dobbin

ACROSS

1 Catchphrase of announcer Harry Caray
8 Early French settler
15 Locale in a 1964 Stan Getz hit
16 Toyota model
17 *Football club that plays at San Siro
18 *First soft drinks sold in cans
19 *Green Lantern company
21 Comedy routine
22 Former Toyota model
25 Big name in ice cream
26 Word of choice
27 Green prefix
28 Painters' degs.
31 Bygone sports org. for which Minnesota governor Jesse Ventura was a TV analyst
33 *He said "Start every day off with a smile and get it over with"
35 Space launch vehicle
39 Contemporary of Luther
40 Report
42 G.P.A. booster
43 *Big clothing retailer
44 Airport announcement, for short
46 Prefix with magnetic
47 Phoenix-to-Albuquerque dir.
48 Unregistered sort
51 Cousin of a dune buggy, for short
53 Observes a religious holiday, in a way
55 Santa ___
56 *Baggy pants popularizer in the 1980s
59 *The Wolfpack, informally
61 Punny title for this puzzle that's a hint to the answers to the starred clues
65 Mrs. ___ cow
66 Remove, as an unnecessary line
67 Give a makeover
68 "Gigi" novelist

DOWN

1 The Company, for short
2 Lines at a store, for short
3 Whack!
4 Indirectly derogatory
5 Sign of hospitality
6 G3, G4 or G5
7 Product from the maker of the 6-Down
8 Bad-smelling
9 Tailbone
10 Jump shots have them
11 Whoop-de-___
12 "That's amazing!"
13 French actor Delon
14 Vicious, as the weather
20 What a slob leaves
22 Smallish bird
23 Capital of Ghana
24 Where houseguests may sleep
26 John of London
29 Swine ___
30 Parts of some campaigns
32 Villainy personified
34 "The best ___ to come"
36 Crescent shapes
37 Regarding
38 Eyelid problems
40 Crackerjack
41 Some chest-thumping, for short
43 World's most populous island
45 "Innocent," but not "guilty"
48 "Jane Eyre" locale
49 Paul McCartney's Albert, e.g.
50 Zaps, in a way
52 "Who are ___ people?!"

by Peter Wentz

54 Rocky ridge
56 Figure in a crèche
57 Fraction of a min.
58 "Love ___"

60 Gang identifier, for short
62 Word after waste or want

63 Well-muscled, informally
64 Véronique, e.g.: Abbr.

ACROSS
1 With 40-Across, a chorus line . . . or a hint to this puzzle's theme
4 Astronomer's accessory
10 Where dolphins perform tricks
14 A fresh start?
15 Painter of many nudes
16 Kind of sandwich
17 Snack on a stick
19 Capital city on the Daugava River
20 ___ de Margarita
21 Imports, as elevator music
23 The Treaty of Versailles ended it
27 Hebdomadally
28 Southeast Asian language
29 Campus org. for ensigns-in-training
31 Oto neighbors
35 Turnips, e.g.
40 See 1-Across
42 Chug
43 Punctual
44 Cover many subjects?
46 Sigma follower
47 Prefix with lineal
51 Secret, e.g.
55 Drive mad
57 Just
58 Lo ___
59 Oscar-winning song from "Aladdin"
64 It might come off the shelf
65 Customize for
66 "Has Anybody Seen My ___?" (1920s song)
67 Europe, Asia and Africa
68 First in an order
69 ___ 10 (acne-fighting medicine)

DOWN
1 Part of many a firm's name
2 ___ Party
3 Young fellow
4 Lovers' plan
5 Long-running MTV show, with "The"
6 Hocked
7 Result of rampant inflation?
8 Like some safety boots
9 Eins + zwei
10 Thread holder
11 Beethoven honoree
12 ___ Doggie (old cartoon pooch)
13 Group making billion-dollar loans
18 Insult, slangily
22 Arizona and Arizona State joined it in '78
23 Parade part
24 "___ dead!"
25 Is peripatetic
26 Orchestrate
30 In ___ (altogether)
32 Experiences
33 Apollo 11 astronaut
34 Plum look-alike
36 Old PC part
37 Indian sauce with coriander and cumin
38 "___ River"
39 Il ___ (it rains: Fr.)
41 Realm of many searches
45 "I've had enough!"
47 Jumbo beginning?
48 Slippery as ___
49 Place for a yellow ribbon
50 1970 Hugo Award-winning novel by Larry Niven
52 Shoulder muscles, for short
53 Many people like to take these apart
54 Nicktoons character
56 Lady ___
60 Old Testament book before Zephaniah: Abbr.

by Julian Lim

61 Bighead
62 Floor cover
63 Possessing much life
experience

ACROSS

1 Pieces of mail
6 Watson's creator
9 Lots
14 *Features accompanying the comics, often
15 What a baby may be
16 *Like some tennis volleys
17 Atlas go-with
19 Legendary racing name
20 Blue-pencil
21 Grimm boy
23 Nashville sch.
24 Iceman Phil or Tony
26 H.S. excellence exam
28 Mined matter
29 John Jacob ___
30 Option after a transmission failure
34 Stalls
37 "Well, did you ___?!"
38 Out of sorts . . . or what completes the answers to the nine starred clues
40 Suffix with senior
41 Sweet breakfast pastry
43 "___ he-e-ere!"
45 Jewish wedding rings?
46 Radiologist's tool, briefly
47 Something to sing over and over
49 Ad come-on, redundantly
54 Boat propeller
55 Double curve
57 Inter ___
58 Beethoven's "___ Solemnis"
60 Makers of knockoffs
62 *Labradoodle, e.g.
63 Capital of Japan
64 *Symbol on some flags
65 Davis of Hollywood
66 Couples' place?
67 Rub off

DOWN

1 "Gosh, you shouldn't've"
2 *Intersection
3 Bygone U.S. Postal Service mascot
4 Keats's "___ Psyche"
5 Q–U string
6 Dream up
7 Good, to Guillermo
8 Cousteau's milieux
9 Forms
10 Reason not to do something
11 Cause for budget cutting
12 *Appear as Tootsie, e.g.
13 Parade
18 Low-quality
22 Life of Riley
25 Favorite ___
27 Fields of comedy
29 Olympics competitor of NZL
30 Union foe
31 Garden evictee
32 Upright swimmers
33 Fielding flaw
34 *Weapon for William Tell
35 Novy ___ (Russian literary magazine)
36 Guadalajara-to-Mexico City dir.
39 Dorm figs.
42 Campaign
44 Rush
46 Steve Buscemi's role in "Reservoir Dogs"
47 Two-for-one, e.g.
48 *Scope lines
49 Hall-of-___
50 Swamp thing
51 Actress Massey
52 *Bygone Chryslers
53 Cup of Cannes
56 Informal greeting
59 Six, in Sicilia
61 Former justice Fortas

by Paula Gamache

ACROSS

1 2007 Ellen Page film
5 Some coolant fluids, for short
9 Runaway success
14 Work on ___ (sunbathe)
15 Da capo ___
16 One leaving a personnel director's office, maybe
17 Study of trees?
19 Dana of "MacGyver"
20 Better halves
21 Henry who founded Cadillac
22 Tenacity
25 Doctrine
28 French comment that may elicit the reply "de rien"
29 Passport for foreign travel, e.g.
30 Article with an ushiromigoro
33 Dinar spender
35 Suits
36 Mic holders
37 Move at all
41 They're on haciendas
43 Persistent Seuss character
44 "Forever, ___" (1996 humor book)
47 Rise
49 Where Spike Lee earned his M.F.A.
50 Survey staple
54 Depletes
55 Orthodontic add-ons
59 Moving about
60 Like the six longest answers in this puzzle
62 Spanish citrus fruit
63 Role in "Hook"
64 Scottish Gaelic name for Scotland
65 Composer Camille Saint-___
66 Red letters?
67 Furniture wood

DOWN

1 Pricey cars, informally
2 Sch. with the mascot Paydirt Pete
3 Prefix with technology
4 Extra life, in a video game
5 City gained by Rome during the First Punic War
6 La ___, Wis.
7 Highly successful
8 Perhaps
9 Unqualified
10 Long time
11 Esoteric
12 Event for a rapper?
13 Drove together
18 Sugar suffix
21 Speaker of the line "Help me, Obi-Wan Kenobi. You're my only hope"
23 Explorer born around A.D. 970
24 TV accessories
25 Five-star W.W. II hero, informally
26 Large roll
27 Fr. title
31 Event
32 Org. associated with U.S. Cyber Command
34 Shooters' grp.?
36 Word before and after "a"
38 Bedlam let loose
39 John who wrote "The Beggar's Opera"
40 Prey for a dingo
42 LP problem
43 Prop in "Cinderella"
44 Is, in math
45 More than one-ninth of the earth's land
46 "Let's get together"
48 Highland girls
51 Goes bad
52 Charlotte of "The Facts of Life"
53 Fanfare
56 International magazine founded in France in 1945

by Neville Fogarty

57 Single-mom sitcom of the 2000s

58 Its state sport is rodeo: Abbr.

60 The Spartans, briefly

61 Pre-texting texts, for short

ACROSS

1 Townsman in "Fiddler on the Roof"
6 Agenda item
10 Does laps, maybe
14 Quarter Pounder topper
15 City founded by King Harald III
16 Per
17 What company bosses do for employees?
19 What comes as a relief?: Abbr.
20 Wonder
21 Hexagonal state
22 Trimmed
23 Best meal of a cow's life?
26 Fox or ox
29 Flatow of NPR
30 ___-American
31 Star followers
33 With 56-Across, a Monopoly order
37 Having a successful theater career?
40 Christmas
41 Virginie, par exemple
42 Like the décor in '50s-themed diners
43 Suffix with personal
44 Has a hunch

45 Guantánamo and others?
51 Build up
52 Hindi relative
53 Center of a Trivial Pursuit board
56 See 33-Across
57 The second round of betting, for one?
60 Common enemy in Dungeons & Dragons
61 Declare
62 Went like molasses
63 Great American Ball Park team
64 Pink-slips
65 Requires

DOWN

1 Parks in Alabama
2 Once more
3 Fisher's wish
4 Autonomous computer program
5 Barbaric
6 Birthstone for most Scorpios
7 Japanese beer brand
8 Tricky
9 Stats in Street Fighter
10 "Aladdin" villain
11 Strauss's "Die Fledermaus," for one
12 Mr. Addams of "The Addams Family"

13 Garden tool
18 Citation abbreviation
22 Green org.?
23 Menotti title character
24 Comment to one who's retiring, informally
25 Sandpaper surface
26 Alternative name for 1st Street, often
27 ___ other (uniquely)
28 Itty-bitty biter
31 Kind of saw
32 ___ Khan
33 Streams often run through them
34 Cereal staple
35 Phoenician port
36 Bears, in Bolivia
38 Iran's ___ Shah Pahlavi
39 Hunt for, as game
43 "___ party time!"
44 Baghdad's ___ City
45 Big-time
46 JPEG, e.g.
47 Scottish landowner
48 Kauai and others
49 Home to nearly 600 miles of the Alaska Highway
50 Makes, as beer
53 Smog
54 Not mint
55 Some are kings and queens

by Eshan Mitra

57 ____-Man
58 Czech surname
   suffix
59 Garden tool

ACROSS

1 Veers quickly
5 Be aware of
9 Breakfast cereal with a propeller-headed alien on the front of the box
14 "Mmm-hmm"
15 Part of a foot
16 Before
17 One sharing an apartment
19 Rhône feeder
20 Daddy Warbucks's henchman
21 "Chow down!"
23 Eastern dance-drama
26 City near Vance Air Force Base
27 Facilities housing large planes?
31 Title in S. America
33 Poles, e.g.
35 Online financial services company
39 Tower, of a sort
40 Actress Parsons
42 One of the Muses
43 Film for which Lee Marvin won Best Actor
45 Pre-C.I.A. org.
47 Captain's log detail
48 Flanged structural element
51 1942 Tommy Dorsey hit with Frank Sinatra vocals
53 Big Irish cream brand
55 Event after a bowl game win
60 Coppola subject
61 Engagement precursor
64 Hoard
65 T.A.E. part
66 Highest point
67 D'Oyly ___ Opera Company
68 Droids, etc.
69 Word that can precede each set of circled letters, forming a literal hint for entering certain answers in this puzzle

DOWN

1 Bad mark in school?
2 Approximation ending
3 "Wow!"
4 Main
5 City near Entebbe airport
6 Sight-seeing grp.?
7 Calendar mo.
8 Marine snail
9 Give out
10 Opened
11 Coast-to-coast route, informally
12 Phone voice?
13 Stated one's case
18 Ones on top of the world?
22 German treat
24 Mont ___
25 Mil. branch
27 Saharan
28 Violinist Leopold
29 F.D.R. initiative
30 Driver
32 Spa, for one
34 Sorrento seven
36 Suffix with plug
37 Frequently
38 ___ Galerie, art museum on Manhattan's Fifth Avenue
41 Five-time U.S. Open winner
44 Set as a price
46 Farm pen
48 Desktop brand
49 Rival of Ole Miss
50 Light years off
52 Record abbr.
54 Allay
56 Eastern rule
57 "The Simpsons" character
58 Blue, say: Abbr.
59 The "2" in x2: Abbr.

by Jules P. Markey

62 Erstwhile
63 Institution
   founded by Thos.
   Jefferson

ACROSS

1 Hawaiian entree
9 "___-Koo" (old ragtime standard)
15 Emphatic call from the flock
16 And others
17 Honoring at a banquet, say
18 Scotland's Loch ___
19 Natal native
20 50th state's bird
22 Kind of sandwich
23 First-year J.D. student
24 Street child
25 Like the area around an erupting volcano
26 Rock layers
28 Tennis whiz
30 One in la familia
31 One concerned about charges
33 Alter
35 Assumes, as costs
38 The Lizard constellation
40 Ones on the move
41 President ___
43 Bow shape
44 Redheaded boy of 1960s TV
46 Bouquets
50 Hard to find in Latin?
52 Cure again, as leather
54 All-night party
55 Sacked out
56 "The Heat ___"
57 Modern home of ancient Elam
58 Batman's home
60 Being borrowed by
63 Pupil surrounder
64 1997 Carrey comedy
65 Spanky or Alfalfa
66 Words after "Que"

DOWN

1 Seder servings
2 Check figure
3 Doctor, ideally
4 Asbestos, for one
5 Dojo floor covering
6 Burgundy bud
7 Skin colorer
8 Former world heavyweight champion Johansson
9 ___ Curtis, onetime cosmetics giant
10 "How was ___ know?"
11 Home of MacDill Air Force Base
12 Part of many a convent
13 Comment made while elbowing someone
14 "And so on"
21 Violinmaker Amati
24 Raiment
27 Many a classical sculpture
29 Soapbox derby entrant
32 Glimpses
34 Some anniversary events
35 Petri dish gel
36 South Pacific island
37 Generates, as fluids
39 ___ early age
42 Modernizes, as a factory
45 First
47 1964 Hitchcock thriller
48 2009 James Cameron blockbuster
49 Madrid madam
51 Like some committees
53 Musical with the song "N.Y.C."
59 Indicator of how something is done
61 Actress ___ Park Lincoln
62 ___ pro nobis

by Kevin Adamick

ACROSS

1 Cheap wheels, perhaps
8 Afghan power
15 Wigged out
16 Going-away request
17 Jazz trumpeter Sandoval and others
18 Peter and Annette of film
19 1960s teaching focus
20 Response to a polite refusal
21 It's spelled out in a Tammy Wynette hit
22 "Steady ___ goes"
25 Looks for oneself, in a way
30 ___ motel
32 What a walk in the ballpark will get you
33 It's spelled out in an Aretha Franklin hit
34 First satellite to transmit a phone call through space, 1962
38 Cold showers
42 Help board a plane, say
44 Young partner
45 It's spelled out in a Travis Tritt hit
46 Connecticut city on the Quinnipiac River
50 Hard work
54 Pull off
55 It's not for big shots
56 Electrical device that may blow
57 Paul Anka hit with a rhyming title
58 Salsa quality
59 Beginning

DOWN

1 Like part of Lake Victoria
2 Not losing well
3 Interweave
4 Te ___
5 Niña or Pinta
6 "There's ___ of gold . . ."
7 Do some farrier's work on
8 Club not seen much nowadays
9 Class for budding painters
10 Den member
11 Midori and Lance
12 Creed
13 ___ Straw Poll
14 Get a home in order
23 A bit, informally
24 Gown go-with
26 Enter the draft, maybe
27 Matches
28 Hot Wheels product
29 Small paving stones
31 Military transports: Abbr.
35 It runs by the White House
36 Mr. Ellington, in a 1977 song
37 Sorry bunch?
39 Asian land where French is widely spoken
40 Makes a 43-Down of
41 Fire starter?
43 Nog flavorer
46 Netting
47 Big show
48 Confident cry
49 Nantes seasons
51 "All ___!" (court cry)
52 General feeling
53 Former capital of Romania

by Joe Krozel

ACROSS
1 Best Picture of 2005
6 Homework-time prohibition
10 Vow words
13 1978 Nicolette Larson hit "___ Love"
14 To the back
16 Cook like the Colonel
17 John who's now a Sir
18 "The Fast and the Furious" co-star
20 Player of 36-/39-Across
22 Global conquest board game
23 Keanu Reeves's character in "The Matrix"
24 Fix, as a drive
28 So far
29 Place for a revolving ball, maybe
31 See 45-Across
32 Sitter's charge
33 Paddle
35 Grandma, affectionately
36 & 39 Jedi master first seen on 5/25/77
41 Tough guy
42 Scatter, as seed
44 Currency board abbr.
45 With 31-Across, favored weapon of 36-/39-Across
47 Father-and-son Hollywood duo

49 "Rock Center" network
52 Figured the price of
54 MGM roarer
55 Zhivago's love
56 Player of 36-/39-Across
59 Temporary transport from a garage
62 Pessimist's plaint
63 Not to mention
64 Gawk
65 Vice President John Garner's middle name
66 Crossed (out)
67 Not go for at all
68 What a napkin may catch

DOWN
1 Children's writer Beverly
2 Relief pitcher Fingers
3 Swear
4 Cattle, e.g.
5 Pend
6 Combatants at Trafalgar
7 River past Ciudad Bolivar
8 Home state of Andrew Johnson: Abbr.
9 See 53-Down
10 Hypothetical cases
11 Rap's Dr. ___
12 Castor ___ of the comics
15 Reacts to leaven
19 Univision interviews are conducted in it

21 The Colts retired his #19
25 Simple rhyme scheme
26 Caesar's "I came"
27 The "E" in B.C.E.
29 Styrofoam maker
30 Barrel material
32 Constrict
34 Blitz, in football
36 Answer to the old riddle "What's round on the sides and high in the middle?"
37 Perturbs
38 ___ pros. (court record abbr.)
40 Figs.
41 Mom's "healing touch"
43 World's largest retailer
46 Lauren of "The Love Boat"
48 Issuance of Pontius Pilate, e.g.
49 1998 Winter Olympics site
50 Mile High player
51 OPEC, e.g.
53 With 9-Down, villain faced by 36-/39-Across
55 Renault model of the 1970s–80s
57 Final Four org.
58 Watermelon hull
59 So-called "Gateway to the Pacific Rim," informally
60 Undivided
61 Put on

by Eric Williams

ACROSS

1 Maker of bonds
5 Oscar nomination, e.g.
10 Hardly a high-rent district
14 Ticket option
15 Bowl
16 Part of the earth
17 65 + 20
19 Unreturnable, in a way
20 City of Syria
21 Very quickly
23 Common drain clogger
25 Payment guarantee
26 Certain pious Jew
29 1-Across plus or minus?
32 Pipe holder
35 "___, I am dying beyond my means": Oscar Wilde
36 Language with only 14 letters
38 Music genre
39 Block
40 75 + 20
41 London facilities
42 "___-comin'!"
43 Key work?
44 Send to the canvas
45 It may be found on a drum
47 ___ Chex
48 Signs of amor
49 Bring (out)

51 See 63-Down
53 Carpentry item in a common simile
57 Swells
61 Bart's teacher
62 1969 Cream hit . . . or a hint to the seven "mathematical" clues in this puzzle
64 Couple
65 Cold war flashpoint
66 Sarcastic reply
67 Hot corner Yank
68 Youngest golfer to shoot his age (67) in a P.G.A. Tour event
69 Kind of column

DOWN

1 Jessica of "Fantastic Four"
2 Slave
3 Figure in "Jack and the Beanstalk"
4 55 + 40
5 Capital known in literature as Thang Long
6 Society: Abbr.
7 ___ Grape
8 Put ___ act
9 Of a branch
10 Tackle box item
11 5 + 10
12 "Trinity" novelist
13 Jungle camping supply

18 Apple tablet
22 Apple on iTunes
24 Commercial district
26 Something that's often best broken
27 Thrifty competitor
28 35 + 10
30 29 + 80
31 Fair-sized musical groups
33 Bygone gas brand
34 Quiet reading spots
36 RR stop
37 $ dispenser
40 Man with a rod, in the Bible
44 75 + 94
46 Picking up the dry cleaning, e.g.
48 You can hardly see it
50 Tire deflaters
52 Syrian strongman
53 ___ vu
54 Effluvium
55 Wood alternative
56 Legends
58 "Welcome Back, Kotter" role
59 First place
60 Fast "birds"
63 Potential source of 51-Across

ACROSS

1 TV sitcom boy who liked to fish
5 Theater prize
9 Essence
14 See 40-Across
16 63-Across, for one
17 With 38- and 59-Across, typical opinion about a record on 40-/14-Across
19 Nautical hazard
20 Flop
21 Subject of a hanging without a trial
22 African capital
24 Miscalculate
26 Grp. on a raid
29 Org. in Robert Ludlum novels
30 Catherine I of Russia, e.g.
34 Labor leader Cesar
36 World's Oldest ___ (nickname for 63-Across)
37 Prefix with flop
38 See 17-Across
39 Juicy fruit
40 With 14-Across, long-running TV show popularized by 63-Across
43 Buffalo's Mets-affiliated team

45 "Buck Rogers" and others
46 Prevailed
47 Cologne compass point
48 "Is that ___?"
49 Little squealer?
51 Many a beneficiary
53 Ebb
55 Former Giants QB Phil
59 See 17-Across
62 Step in
63 Late beloved TV personality
64 Audibly stunned
65 Saloon choices
66 Genesis figure

DOWN

1 Tokyo ties
2 Lane
3 ___ many words
4 Award for mystery writers
5 Giant who swung for the fences
6 Start of a children's rhyme
7 Gold bar
8 Biblical land whose name means "red" in Hebrew
9 King or queen
10 Cause to blush, maybe
11 Cake finisher

12 In order
13 Understand
15 Comfort
18 Too weighty
23 Hollywood, with "the"
25 Bled
26 Pretend to be
27 With 51-Down, "14-Across Boogie," on 40-/14-Across
28 Sea follower?
30 ___ Talks (idea presentations)
31 Nanook's home
32 Las Vegas signs
33 "Give it ___!"
35 Zoning board issues
36 C&W channel, once
38 Standard batteries
41 Actor McShane
42 Funny one
43 Heckle, in a way
44 Right away
46 From what place
49 ___ mail
50 King or queen
51 See 27-Down
52 "I'm ___ here!"
54 "___ little sugar" (recipe directive)
56 Complain
57 A Barcelona museum is dedicated to his work
58 Nasdaq listings: Abbr.

by David J. Kahn

59 Vote of approval
60 Dada pioneer
61 Bank printings:
   Abbr.

ACROSS

1 Massage treatment
8 Intense conflict
14 Fruit salad item
15 Rich, cheddary party food
16 Banking aid
17 Wall art
18 Future atty.'s exam
19 Charges may be made with these
21 Lead-in to "ops"
22 "Holiday" actor Ayres
23 Bird with a mythological name
24 Some people kneel in front of it
26 Numbing, in a way
27 Amount of space in a paper to be filled with journalism
32 A Trump
35 Year Christopher Columbus died
36 "Hey, what's going ___ there?"
37 N.L. home run king until Willie Mays surpassed him in 1966
38 Ancient measure
39 Certain wildcat
40 It may get in a jam
41 Nebraska county whose seat is Nebraska City
42 Shoots out
43 Snack on the go
45 ___-de-Calais (French department)
46 Keyboard key
47 Grand
49 Water source
52 Wee amphibian
55 Tendencies
57 Noodle ___
58 Onetime White House family
60 Not yet caught
62 Moves
63 Camp employee
64 Hybrid articles of apparel
65 Green, in a way

DOWN

1 Trivial
2 Provider of hints
3 Many a holiday visitor
4 Help in wrongdoing
5 Blacken
6 Like water in a moving tank
7 Parts of arms
8 Dorothy Parker attribute
9 Sometimes they're perfect
10 Rule, briefly
11 Nile deity
12 It's a crime
13 Bakers' supply
15 "Evita" role
20 Cylindrical cardboard containers apropos for this puzzle?
23 Record company with a lightning bolt in its logo
25 "My bad!"
26 Really digging something
28 1960s singer Sands
29 Some time ago
30 Hide out
31 Tolkien tree creatures
32 "___ the end of my rope!"
33 Velvety pillow cover
34 Start for boy or girl
35 Conductor Riccardo
38 Farm machines
42 Pollen holder
44 Canada's largest brewery
45 Engine part
48 "Shalom"
49 Trunk
50 Poet with a role in "Roots"
51 Fishing spots
52 Goes astray
53 "You all right?"
54 ___ Bell

by Elizabeth C. Gorski

56 Fool
57 Eastern royal
59 Air-gulping fish
61 Hon

ACROSS

1 With 65-Across, part of a record . . . or what each of this puzzle's five long Across answers has?
5 Actress Knightley
10 "___, vidi, vici"
14 Prefix with sphere
15 Get all A's
16 Big name in paperback publishing
17 Puerto Rico, affectionately, with "the"
20 Last Whig president
21 Mixologist's unit
22 Basketball Hall of Fame coach Hank
23 What the Mars symbol symbolizes
25 Malady named after a Connecticut town
30 Does a pre-laundry chore
31 Rapa ___ (locale of many monoliths)
32 Stereo parts
36 London's West End, e.g.
40 Repairs, as a golf green
41 What makes Shrek shriek?
42 ___-Loompa (chocolate factory dwarf)
43 Record collector's curio
46 City with a U.F.O. museum

50 Jet ___
51 Stop, as a launch
52 State with just three counties
57 Lucasfilm aircraft
60 "Ah, 'twas not to be"
61 Big name in coffeemakers
62 Righty Hershiser
63 Arts and Sciences dept.
64 Sumptuous fur
65 See 1-Across

DOWN

1 Feudal estate
2 Actress Anderson
3 With: Abbr.
4 Science fiction writer Frederik
5 Obi-Wan ___
6 Over 300,000 of these appear in "Gandhi"
7 Frozen beverage brand
8 Like a matador's cape
9 Successor of Muhammad, to Shiites
10 Appraiser's figure
11 Maiden name of Harry Potter's mother
12 Present occasion
13 Rear of many a book
18 In the heart of
19 Only
23 Wailuku is its county seat

24 Sale tag condition
25 W.W. II naval vessels: Abbr.
26 Disney tune subtitled "A Pirate's Life for Me"
27 TV star who homered off Koufax in a 1963 episode
28 Airport postings, for short
29 Bring a relationship to a close
32 Yankees' #13, to fans
33 "La Bohème" role
34 Psychedelic drugs, for short
35 Quick and detached, in mus.
37 Train travel
38 Abbr. on the bottom of a business letter
39 Morgue ID
43 Animals with collars, often
44 Of service
45 Winterize, as a coat
46 Indian ruler
47 Printing daggers
48 Cokes and such
49 Pulse-taking spot
52 Dull
53 "___ calling?"
54 Longfellow bell town
55 Clarinetist's need
56 Writer ___ Stanley Gardner

by Gary Cee

58 Conan O'Brien's network

59 Celestial altar

ACROSS

1 Brewer Coors
7 Add liberally to
13 & 14 With 64-Across, familiar rule not always followed
15 5-Down and others
17 Da's opposite
18 Bygone record label
19 Melodramatic sound
20 Adobes and abodes
22 Touchdown stat
24 Twins sharing a star on the Hollywood Walk of Fame
27 Push to the right, say
30 Part of an extended family
31 Chem. assay
32 China problem
35 Cap
37 It's good for your health
39 Automaker Ferrari
40 QB calls
42 ___ Tales, magazine where many H. P. Lovecraft stories first appeared
43 Ban on strip mining, e.g.
45 Western and foreign, to moviegoers
46 Chess piece: Abbr.
47 "___ want to talk about it"
49 Be behind
52 Relaxes
54 Fordham athletes
58 Studier of distant emissions
61 Major
62 Ones giving cash for quarters
63 Some Rijksmuseum holdings
64 See 13-Across

DOWN

1 "It's ___!"
2 Take out
3 Not paid for, as factory work
4 One to build on
5 Some charitable sporting events
6 Part of un jour
7 How some argue
8 One who's split
9 Pal
10 Authors
11 Vision: Prefix
12 Investigator of many accidents, for short
13 Engine part: Abbr.
14 Northern extremes?
16 Mr. Mojo ___ (anagrammatic nickname for Jim Morrison)
21 "That's ___ hadn't heard"
23 Subject of a six-volume history by Edward Gibbon
24 "Going ___ . . ."
25 Property claim
26 Lay claim to
28 Informal turndowns
29 Its for more than one
31 It flows in un río
33 Brief start
34 Ones hoofing it
36 Stars and others
38 Rocker Stefani
41 Plot feature
44 Temporarily out, say
45 Disappear
48 Sorghum variety
49 Stars, e.g.
50 Checkout line complaint
51 Kind of piece in a jigsaw puzzle
53 Literary monogram
55 Ascap part: Abbr.
56 Bobcat or Cougar, for short
57 Class that's soon to leave: Abbr.
59 Suffix with opal
60 Sarcasm clarifier

by Joe Krozel

ACROSS

1 California valley
5 It may be cut by an uppercut
8 Off-mike remarks
14 Counting of the ___ (observance after Passover)
15 Prefix with skeleton
16 Totally confused
17 *Staffing level
19 Flu sufferer's quaff
20 Montezuma's people
21 Spout forth, as venom
23 Mid 11th-century year
24 Handed out
25 *Refuse to cooperate
27 Protein-rich bean
29 Revolutionary killed in his bathtub
30 It's taken before a shot
33 Takeout container size
35 "Axis of evil" member
38 Inviting danger . . . the end of which can precede each half of the answer to each asterisked clue
43 Tijuana's peninsula
44 Peak in "The Odyssey"
45 Marked, in a way
46 Name in garden products
50 Singer with lowercase initials
52 *Woodcraft hobbyist's creation
55 Horse of the Year, 1960–64
59 A, in Arles
60 Muddy up
61 Like the Best Picture of 2011
62 Mucho
64 *Toothless mammal
66 Zippo filler
67 Word on Italian street signs
68 "Comin' ___ the Rye"
69 Likkered up
70 Flow back
71 Ref. works sometimes sold with magnifying glasses

DOWN

1 One without roots
2 Blow away
3 Numerical prefix
4 Van Cleef & ___ (French jeweler)
5 Moe, Larry and Curly, ethnically
6 Wood splitter
7 Least skillful
8 Parthenon goddess
9 Prebirth event
10 N.Y.C.'s first subway
11 Obsolescent printer type
12 Tom of "The Seven Year Itch"
13 Creature with one foot
18 Prey for moray eels
22 Fluffy lap dog, for short
25 Violated the "code of silence"
26 Street urchin
28 Yang's opposite
30 Alert for the squad, for short
31 Dockworkers' org.
32 Baton wielder
34 1955 Thunderbird seating capacity
36 Lionel Richie's "You ___"
37 Proof letters
39 Sale locale
40 Part of a chain
41 J.F.K. inits.
42 Tearjerker watcher's item
47 Homophone of 16-Across
48 Walked, with "it"
49 Vote in Parlement
51 Cold dessert
52 Nursery purchases
53 Bidirectional, like a door
54 Work like a dog

by Susan Gelfand

56 River of Hades
57 Dummy Mortimer
58 Others, in
Oaxaca

61 Wild guess
63 It has teeth but
no mouth
65 Penpoint

80 MEDIUM

ACROSS

1 Blue
4 "M*A*S*H" extra
9 Controls
14 San Francisco's ___ Valley
15 Kind of skeleton
16 Cravat alternative
17 Bergman's 1956 Oscar-winning role
19 Siberian native
20 -
21 Boglike
23 Had something
24 Twists
26 -
28 ___ Schwarz
30 H. G. Wells race
32 Humans and ostriches
33 "___ you something"
35 Supreme Court groupings
37 -
39 EarthLink, e.g., for short
40 Calligraphy detail
44 Airway
47 Dam's companion
48 "Camptown Races" composer
51 -
53 "Yikes!"
54 Incorrect reasoning
56 "Thus ___ the Lord"
58 Ring of plumerias
59 Casual denials

61 Hydrogen has one
64 Yemeni port
66 Umber or ocher
68 Drug-free
69 1980 Tony Award-winning musical
70 A.T.M. manufacturer
71 -
72 -
73 -

DOWN

1 Percussion in a marching band
2 Bang-up
3 Nonessentials
4 Ripen
5 Aid for clarity
6 Slam
7 "___ to please"
8 Co-star of Showtime's "Homeland"
9 Cricket relatives
10 Code-cracking org.
11 89 or 91, maybe
12 Went by sound, perhaps
13 Italicize, e.g.
18 Madrid Mrs.
22 Former sitcom featuring a #1 singer
25 Kind of wave
27 Some places to pray
28 Gung-ho

29 Cause of some wrinkles
31 Tattered
34 All, in music
36 Pentathlon equipment
38 Full of life?
41 Legal maneuver . . . with a hint to answering seven clues in this puzzle
42 Roth ___
43 Agent of Uncle Sam
45 What the fat lady sings?
46 Learn to live with
48 Actor's screen recognition
49 Corrida chant
50 Sectioned
52 When repeated, 1968 name in the news
55 Rooted for
57 "Sesame Street" watcher
60 Goalkeeper's glory
62 Erstwhile
63 Dweeb
65 Japanese "yes"
67 Purge

by Tracy Gray

ACROSS

1 Title matchmaker of early 19th-century literature
5 Drifting type
9 Some help
14 With 21-Across, ship out?
15 Britain's Douglas-Home
16 Need for a 17-Across
17 Special delivery of a sort
20 Fluoride, e.g.
21 See 14-Across
22 Spots for rubs and scrubs
23 Is homesick, say
25 "Oedipe" opera composer, 1936
27 Response to being tickled
29 They often have quiet eyes
32 Moo ___
34 Santa's checking things
36 N.F.L. QB Kyle
37 Revolutionary Tribunal casualty
40 Verdugo of "Marcus Welby, M.D."
41 Oxford attachment?
42 Automne follows it
43 Fort's steep slope
45 Click beetle
47 Go at

49 98.6°, say
52 Korean War outbreak year
54 Starchy
56 African antelope
57 Discovery of Vitus Bering before his shipwreck
60 Paavo ___, track's Flying Finn
61 "Live at Red Rocks" pianist
62 Under tension
63 Some tides
64 City in Padua province
65 Shakespeare title contraction

DOWN

1 Steele work
2 Where "ayuh" is an affirmative
3 What 007 might shoot with
4 He declared "The planet has a fever"
5 Largest ethnic group in China
6 Pasternak mistress Ivinskaya
7 Implicatively
8 Large quantity
9 GPS screen abbr.
10 Curling rink line seven yards from the tee
11 Destination after a touchdown

12 Scholarship-offering org.
13 4-Down's grp.
18 Semicircular canals' locales
19 Burning solutions
24 2008 demolition target
26 Eolith or neolith
28 Fifth of fünf
30 Glam rock's ___ the Hoople
31 Old dagger
32 Hook helper
33 Dutch Golden Age painter
35 Dirty
38 Experiencing down time
39 Home of Sistan and Baluchestan
44 Spanish term of endearment
46 Printed slips
48 Really put out
50 "The X Factor" panelist, once
51 Things Santa checks
52 "Doctor Faustus" novelist
53 Footprint or fingerprint, say
55 Tears can create one
58 "Indeedy"
59 "___ Cried" (1962 hit song)

by Joel Kaplow

82 HARD

ACROSS

1 Navajo terrain
6 Chicken ___
10 Pack member, for short?
13 Top
14 What going 100 might result in
17 "You ___ one"
18 1980s–90s hip-hop show co-hosted by Fab 5 Freddy
19 Ingurgitate
21 Delectable
22 Joins
24 Food item whose name means "pounded"
25 "Patton" setting
27 Relieve
28 They often accompany discoveries
29 Congregation, metaphorically
32 Org. studying viruses
35 Be daring
39 Sound after "Lower . . . lower . . . that's it!"
40 Noted entertainer with a whistle
41 Site of a religious retreat
42 Oaf

43 Sneeze cause
46 Salad bar offering
49 Writer about a bear
51 "Julie & Julia" co-star
53 Amass
56 "Bad for bacteria" brand
58 Setting for the 1996 documentary "When We Were Kings"
59 "Funny People" actor
60 "Pietà or Revolution by Night" artist
61 Jerk
62 Zip
63 "L'Amateur d'estampes" painter

DOWN

1 Subjunctive, e.g.
2 Dutch chess grandmaster Max
3 First N.B.A. player to light the Olympic cauldron
4 Caution
5 French nuns
6 Liberal arts dept.
7 Midway, e.g.
8 Fratricide victim of myth
9 "Meet the ___" (major-league fight song)

10 Bye lines?
11 Data
12 Artist's supply
15 Line at a water fountain, maybe
16 Burned out
20 Échecs piece
23 Modern-day pointer
25 Part of a bar order
26 "Dream on!"
27 King, e.g.: Abbr.
30 Like '40s boppers
31 Colossal, to Coleridge
32 Christmas order
33 Alter ___ amicus
34 Follow
36 It rolls across fields
37 Gorgon, e.g.
38 Business that's always cutting back?
42 Disinclined
44 Put on
45 Like some doughnuts and eyes
46 Makings of a model, maybe
47 Billet-doux recipients
48 Some bump producers
49 Computer that pioneered in CD-ROMs
50 Onetime Moore co-star
52 Longtime Yankee moniker

by Brendan Emmett Quigley and Caleb Madison

54 Nocturnal bear
55 No ___ (store sign)
57 Rhinology expert,
for short

ACROSS

1 Like eaters of humble pie
7 Impossible dream
14 Clichéd company claim
15 Surveilled, say
16 Onetime pickling liquid
17 Pumpkin is rich in it
18 Party makeup?
20 Abbr. accompanying some dotted notes
21 Urban planting favorite
22 Half the time?: Abbr.
25 Makes less edgy
27 A weather strip may fit into it
29 Only Englishman named a Dr. of the Church
32 Tony's "Taras Bulba" co-star, 1962
34 Maneuver
35 Reckon
37 Producer of a blowout, maybe
39 Danny DeVito's "Throw Momma From the Train" role
40 Clock stopper, at times
42 Good dogs for pulling loads
43 Most negligible
45 Expect
47 Winged ___
48 Cobble, perhaps
50 More, in ads
54 Maker of fabrics with intricate designs
56 Tryst figure
59 Running quarterly, for short?
60 A 40-Across will watch for it
61 C3H8, e.g.
62 Like some words and swords
63 Reacted to a punch

DOWN

1 Alternatives to sales
2 Spartan toiler
3 ___ Express
4 What Jack got in exchange for a cow, in a children's story
5 Form of "sum"
6 Proper
7 Attributes (to)
8 Grand entrance?
9 Retort of contradiction
10 Longtime Dodgers coach Manny
11 Feta milk source
12 "Footloose" hero McCormack
13 Ending for AriZona flavors
15 Hardly abundant
19 N.L. Central city
22 Divvy up
23 Cabbage
24 Ocular irritants
26 "Bad" cholesterol, briefly
28 Inscrutable
29 Tiptoed, say
30 Spa handout
31 Subs
33 Body shop offering
36 Cheerleading outfit?
38 A 40-Across may call it
41 Like many bakers' hands
44 Walks heavily
46 Resembling
49 Collège, e.g.
51 Like the Navajo language
52 ABC's Arledge
53 Full of adrenaline
54 Shocks
55 World's largest fruit company
56 One-striper, briefly
57 Swiss stream
58 Spanish stream

by Barry C. Silk and Brad Wilber

ACROSS

1 Fashion show disaster
4 Dated
7 Make a major decision?
9 Head honcho in baseball
11 Element in many semiconductors
13 Like galley slaves, typically
15 Late 1980s Cadillac
16 Literally, "the Stairway"
17 ___ Day
19 Makes a person less tense
20 Exceeds, as demand
21 Closet item, for short
24 Collection of Blaise Pascal writings
25 Middle of this century
28 Spanish queen and namesakes
30 Father-and-son Connecticut congressmen Thomas and Chris
31 Big ring
32 Buckle attachment
34 9–5 connector
35 Choice word?
36 With love
39 Long Island university
40 Like the relatives notified in emergencies, usually
41 Entices
42 Grass for some baskets
43 Economical
44 It might be tipped at a rodeo

DOWN

1 Fingers on a diamond
2 "That's my intention"
3 Quickly reproduces
4 Ship's boarding ladder
5 Keys and Markova
6 CeCe of gospel
7 Lavish events
8 Like John Kerry in 2004
9 Opposites of mansions
10 Food topping in France
11 Blast
12 Has no significance
13 They let traffic through after a crash
14 German article
18 Doesn't continue, as an argument
21 Maintainers of a sacred flame in ancient Rome
22 Made a commitment to play
23 Boxing Hall-of-Famer Primo
25 Sewers, often
26 Sends
27 ___ Hewitt, 2002 Wimbledon winner
29 Nascar driver Elliott
31 Eye
33 One side of a longstanding ad battle
35 Military encampment
37 Nose: Prefix
38 Sign for a musician not to play

by Joe Krozel

85 Hard

ACROSS

1 Stud, say
11 Court defendant: Abbr.
15 He played Don Altobello in "The Godfather Part III"
16 Fair
17 Side effect?
18 Hillbilly's plug
19 More, to a 37-Down
20 Eric of "Funny People," 2009
21 It's gradually shrinking in the Arctic
23 Lost traction
24 One punched in an office
25 Kitchen dusting aid
28 Admirable person
29 They might be left hanging
30 Not pussyfooting
31 1990s Indian P.M.
32 "Youth With a Skull" painter
33 Didn't use a high enough 45-Across, maybe
34 Carpenter's groove
35 Some E.M.T. cases
36 They stand for things
37 Kind of nut
38 Evenly matched

40 Employees at a ritzy hotel
41 Is routed by
42 Whiff
43 Hand holder?
44 Grain, e.g.
45 Ray blockage no.
48 Month whose zodiac sign is a fish
49 "Lady Baltimore" novelist, 1906
52 Prefix with 3-Down
53 "It'll be O.K." lead-in
54 Tummy filler
55 "Whoa, not so fast!"

DOWN

1 Appear thrilled
2 Two before Charlie
3 Computing 0s and 1s
4 Milk source
5 Sense, slangily
6 Aquila's brightest star
7 Secretive body part
8 Mariner's grp.
9 Outer: Prefix
10 Postapocalyptic best seller of 1978
11 Wraps up
12 Send
13 Flighty type
14 Drills, e.g.
22 League division
23 Criteria: Abbr.
24 Veers sharply

25 Friend one grows up with, often
26 "News to me!"
27 Reason for a track delay
28 "Faded Love" singer, 1963
30 Film with the tagline "Borat was SO 2006"
33 Where following a star might lead you
34 Shoulder press target, briefly
36 It's in front of the cockpit
37 South-of-the-border bad guy
39 Colorful additions to tanks
40 Beheld
42 Name in seven Shakespeare titles
44 Charges from counsel
45 They may be prayed to in Fr.
46 Graceful fairy
47 Part of a long neck
50 "Huh?"
51 "___ being Brand" (Cummings poem)

by Ian Livengood

Note: This puzzle has two bonus answers in appropriate places. Can you find them?

ACROSS
1 Big chickens
9 Seat cushions?
15 Loose
16 Like Fiennes's Shakespeare
17 Supply in a camper's first-aid kit
18 Actress Matlin
19 W.W. II inits.
20 British meat pies
22 Soviet accords?
23 Maine's ___ Bay
25 Locks
26 Kind of cloud
27 Vertical: Prefix
28 Anderson who wrote "My Life in High Heels"
29 1950s–60s singer Jackson, the Queen of Rockabilly
30 Forum : Rome :: ___ : Athens
32 Go on
33 Exchange
36 Talking-tos
37 "Save the ___" (conservationists' catchphrase)
38 A park may have one
39 No challenge
40 See 51-Across
41 Stoked
45 Grand
46 Stern contemporary

47 Massey of "Frankenstein Meets the Wolf Man"
48 "This is a test. For the next 60 seconds . . ." org.
49 Beats
51 Notable stat for 40-Across
52 Nickname for Warren Weber in an old sitcom
54 Rowdy
56 "I'm a walking, talking ___": Larry David
57 Resting
58 Bee wine
59 Veteran

DOWN
1 Plain's opposite
2 Commensurate (with)
3 "It's about time!"
4 Doo-wop syllable
5 Grave, for one
6 "Confessions of a Drunkard" writer, 1822
7 Didn't have enough
8 "The Brandenburgers in Bohemia" composer
9 Scrabble accessory
10 Final pharaoh of the Fifth Dynasty, whose pyramid is near Cairo

11 Canon type, briefly
12 Retain
13 Classic actress who played the principal in "Grease"
14 Reel
21 Junior Jr.
24 Hat
26 Dish eaten with a spoon
28 "___ on First" (1981 comedian's biography)
29 Tune (up)
31 Hiking snack
32 Aid consideration
33 Big house
34 Offensive formation
35 Uncommitted
36 Sacagawea, for one
38 "In actuality . . ."
40 Minnesota senator Klobuchar
42 Homer's "dread monster"
43 Not home?
44 Picked up
46 Gossip opening
47 Key chain?
49 Italian lyrical verse
50 N.F.L. coach Jim
53 ___ Friday
55 Bit of news in the financial sect.

by Matt Ginsberg

ACROSS

1 Cuisine featuring nam prik
5 Identifies
9 Counterpart
13 Mezzo-soprano Marilyn
15 1968 Best Actor nominee for "The Fixer"
17 A blimp may hover over one
18 Induce squirming in, perhaps
19 Coat that's easy to take off
21 French loanword that literally means "rung on a ladder"
22 Colors
24 Perfect
25 It was MSNBC's highest-rated program when canceled in 2003
26 Antique shop purchase
29 Wizard's garment
30 Paper assets
36 Device with a hard disk
37 It has a denomination of $1,000
38 Homeric character who commits matricide
41 Weapons used to finish off the Greek army at Thermopylae
46 What a robot might resemble
47 To the left
48 Psychedelic 1968 song featuring a lengthy drum solo
51 What a whatnot has
52 Like molasses
53 Danger for a climber
54 President's daughter on "The West Wing"
55 Alternative to "your"
56 Company whose Nasdaq symbol is the company's name
57 Keep alive, as a fire

DOWN

1 Showed a bit more friendliness
2 Poet who gave us "carpe diem"
3 Singer at Barack's inauguration
4 Poor
5 Hymn sung to Apollo
6 Trees in Gray's country churchyard
7 Kaplan who co-hosted six seasons of "High Stakes Poker"
8 Acknowledge a commander's entrance, maybe
9 Pizza sauce
10 Not going with the flow?
11 Round-bottomed container
12 Letter on Kal-El's costume
14 One hanging at a temple
16 It's all in your head
20 Christmas green?
23 Gets the gist
25 Dimwit
27 "I hate it when that happens!"
28 Business often located near an interstate
30 Obstruct
31 Trunk item
32 Too accommodating for one's own good
33 Once-autonomous people of southern Russia
34 Sober
35 Nonwoody plant parts
39 Senate sheets
40 Make possible
42 Disobey the rule?
43 Baltimore's ___ Park
44 Begin with enthusiasm
45 Got a lot of laughs out of
47 1980s Tyne Daly role

by Patrick Berry

49 Small quantity
50 Surrealism
forerunner
51 Buddy

ACROSS

1 Crowds around noisily
5 "In the Still of the Nite" doo-wop group, with "the"
15 Beginning of time?
16 Somewhat
17 Korean War weapon
18 Where to request a knish
19 "___ the brinded cat hath mewed": Shak.
21 Like sports cars, briefly
22 Reagan-era teen, e.g.
23 Modern-day stream
25 Burgeon
27 Like some shape shifters?
29 Cut bits from, maybe
33 What "-" means in a search query
34 Big ring rivals
36 Mark of a successful gunfighter
37 They cause blowups
39 Like many disabled vehicles
41 Positions
42 Helped supply a sushi restaurant, say
44 Promotions may require them, for short
46 Chile's main airline
47 Yarn identifier

49 Bar lines?
51 Washout
53 First bishop of Paris
54 "Looky here!"
57 ___ balls (chocolaty snacks)
59 1950 sci-fi classic
60 Medium relative
63 Mini successor
64 Spy's query at the start of a meeting
65 LeAnn Rimes's "Love ___ Army"
66 Like legal voters
67 Take out

DOWN

1 Like some top-10 people
2 Like bull's-eyes
3 One in a stag's litter
4 "Aah!"
5 Tricks
6 1969 Peace Prize agcy.
7 Certain stamp of approval
8 Fifth element, per Aristotle
9 Of atoms' spatial relationships
10 The Hebrew Hammer of the Cleveland Indians
11 J.F.K. speechwriter Sorensen

12 Horned mountain dweller
13 View from Memphis
14 Kerfuffle
20 Airport fleet
24 It's south of the Banda Sea
26 Hydroxyl compound
28 Tinkertoy bit
30 One of Henderson's record 1,406
31 Off-and-on
32 Bit of paste
35 2009 Tennis Hall of Fame inductee
38 Common portrait subject
40 Beat
43 Actress-turned-nun Hart
45 Abolhassan Bani-___ (first president of Iran)
48 Clawed
50 Russian playwright Andreyev
52 Guideposts magazine founder
54 "'Tis all a Chequer-board of Nights and Days" poet
55 Take on
56 Universal donor's type, briefly
58 Kitchen drawer?

by Barry C. Silk

61 Traffic violation, for short

62 Okla. City-to-Tulsa direction

ACROSS

1 The miss in "Miss Saigon"
4 Burger go-withs
10 Big race sponsor
13 Dishes fit for astronomers?
16 Panglossian person
17 Asia-to-Africa link
18 Carmen ___ ("The Producers" role)
19 Interior decorator's suggestion
20 Southeast Asian holiday
21 Grp. concerned with bowls
23 Rout
26 Mean cur, typically
28 Ice cream mix-in
30 Place to go in Soho
31 See 32-Across
32 On the 31-Across side
34 ___ question
36 South Asian chant word
38 Had a lot to digest
40 Restless
41 Ear-related
43 Longtime Russian acronym
44 ___ Dogg Pound (rap duo)
45 Chihuahua scratch?
47 Adjust one's sights
49 Lays atop
51 Asset
53 King, in Cape Verde
55 Handy-andy's letters
56 Box-office take
58 SALT I and II, e.g.
60 Beloved "Immortal Beloved" piece
63 How this puzzle's black squares are arranged
64 They may have you in stitches, in brief
65 Gunsmith with Smith
66 One may say "I'm with stupid"

DOWN

1 "Take cover!"
2 Security requests
3 Star in Cetus
4 What an express often whizzes by: Abbr.
5 Hägar's wife
6 Polynesian farewell song
7 "Beau Geste" headgear
8 Responsibility for a groundskeeper
9 Grade sch. subject
10 Round-trip flight?
11 Tackles a tough task
12 W. Coast clock setting
13 Do some recharging
14 Center for cat-tails?
15 Highly decorated Bradley
22 Prefix with many fruit names
24 Georgetown athlete
25 Things worked under in a garage
27 "Sax All Night" New Ager
29 Mtge. broker's come-on
31 "SCTV" lineup
33 Hmong homeland
35 It is in Spain
37 It has a sticking point
39 Sandy shade
42 Pre-stunt provocation
46 Thing worked on in a garage
48 Second-largest city in Finland
50 Matched up, after "in"
52 Can
54 Exeter exclamation
57 Cut takers: Abbr.
59 Some kind of ___
60 6 letters
61 Fan setting
62 Apollo's chariot "passenger"

by Scott Atkinson

ACROSS

1 Gemini, Libra and Aquarius
9 Untrustworthy sort
15 Result of too much TV, it's said
16 Not bad, in Nantes
17 Common aquarium decoration
18 Promotional description for a coming show
19 Ancient key
20 Goat's call
21 "Green Book" org., familiarly
22 Home of the Dostoyevsky Literary Museum
23 Kitchen tool
24 Do stuff
29 Field marshals' commands
30 Thumbs-up
34 Monkey ladder vine
35 Holiday when sweeping and emptying the trash are considered bad luck
36 Vega of "Spy Kids"
37 Polyhedron part
38 Chaotic
40 Symbiotic partners of clownfish
41 "She is more precious than ___": Proverbs 3:15
45 Points
46 Garment originally made from caribou or sealskin
47 "___ Back" (2004 Kenny Chesney hit)
48 Tarzan trademark
52 Takes a powder
53 Steve Allen sidekick with the catchphrase "Hi-ho, Steverino!"
55 Cup alternative
56 Engaged, as a target
57 Keeping half the world down, say
58 Flock member

DOWN

1 "East of Eden" girl
2 Unrelenting
3 Pool accessory
4 Guru follower
5 "___ 500" (annual list)
6 Case study?
7 Cape Breton locale
8 Taco Bell offering
9 Dogs that ought to be great swimmers?
10 State of nervous tension
11 Test course challenges
12 Sphere of influence
13 Old country name or its currency, both dropped in 1997
14 "The Apostles" composer
22 Mrs. Václav Havel, the first first lady of the Czech Republic
24 Game part
25 "Celeste Aida," e.g.
26 Leopard's home?
27 Hall-of-Fame Cub Sandberg
28 Conniving
30 Imperial offering
31 "Smoke Gets in Your Eyes" composer
32 Wheelset piece
33 Exuberant cries
36 Byrd and others: Abbr.
38 Executive suite?
39 Fix up, in a way
40 Nobel-winning poet Heaney
41 Lacks a clear voice
42 "Say ___!"
43 Compound used to kill ants
44 Ramadi resident
48 River intentionally flooded in W.W. I
49 Michael who wrote "The Neverending Story"
50 Home of the international headquarters of Interpol
51 Time of forbearance
54 Reverend ___, onetime radio evangelist

by Byron Walden

ACROSS

1 Many fans are running during this
9 Three-toed wading birds
15 Gets
16 Present-day cry?
17 A vegetarian isn't on it
18 Holds forth
19 Tycoon types
20 "Go ahead," to Shakespeare
21 Certain odor absorber
22 Tabulae ____
23 Storming-out sounds
24 Must-see
27 Spam protection items?
28 Like many bread knives
30 Grammy-winning Brian
31 Looks
32 ____ of Lagery (Pope Urban II's real name)
33 Brushing and such
35 Blood rival
36 Ivy supporters
37 It's developed in a sonata
38 Parts of kingdoms
39 Curtain fabrics
40 Needs for some games of tag
42 Noted 19th- and 20th-century portraitist
43 Flight from danger
44 Bump down
45 Immobilized during winter, say
46 "Not if my life depended on it!"
47 "Done"
48 Four-seaters, maybe?

DOWN

1 Clumsy
2 Queen Mary, for one
3 "Don't do it!"
4 TV Land staple
5 They often get depressed
6 Modern guest-list organizer
7 Onetime Virginia V.I.P.'s
8 Amphibious carrier, for short
9 Establishment where customers typically are seated
10 Singer with the 1994 #1 alternative rock hit "God"
11 Short, strong pan
12 They may be odd
13 Malcolm-Jamal's "Cosby Show" role
14 Plea for aid
20 Teases playfully
22 It hasn't yet been interpreted
24 Strikes out
25 What many crewmen carouse on
26 Deposited into a bank
28 Dancer who was a fan favorite?
29 Ones giving winner forecasts
31 Amass
34 Not belowdecks
35 Tiny biter causing intense itching
37 Sign of availability
39 "Swearin' to God" singer, 1975
40 Hardly a good looker
41 1966 A.L. Rookie of the Year
42 Ward on a set
43 Sock
44 Not quite make the putt, with "out"

by Tim Croce

ACROSS

1 Regular fluctuation
11 Resourcefulness
15 Choose not to mess with
16 Stop shooting
17 Written between two rows of text
18 "But men are men; the best sometimes forget" speaker
19 Opposing
21 "Jelly Roll, Bix and ___" (1994 history of early jazz)
22 Lamb's "___ From Shakespeare"
23 Empty space
24 ___ of Denmark (James I's queen consort)
25 Fiber-rich fruits
26 Madrigal syllables
28 Crumbled ingredient in "dirt pudding"
29 Takes the big cheese down to size?
30 Surprising revelation
34 Superior facility
35 "You have been ___"
36 Salon selections
37 She bests Sherlock in "A Scandal in Bohemia"
38 Light
39 Snide remark
43 Items found in jackets
44 TV golf analyst who won three Masters
46 What tickets may get you
47 Some movies on TV are shown in it
50 Possible solution
51 Approximately
52 Film genre
53 Quick affair?
54 One attracted to vinegar
55 Terrible #2s

DOWN

1 "24" actress Cuthbert
2 Robert who won Oscars for both writing and directing "Kramer vs. Kramer"
3 1942 invasion site
4 Pay back
5 Square
6 "Burning Giraffes in Yellow" painter
7 More obdurate
8 Much earlier
9 Two stars of "Paper Moon"
10 One held in a trap
11 When the O.S.S. was formed
12 Reagan-era scandal
13 Subjects of many notices stapled to telephone poles
14 Part of a timing pattern on a football field
20 Winners of the longest postseason game in major-league history (18 innings, 2005)
25 Lead role in "Miracle on 34th Street"
27 Way to serve vegetables
28 1940s–50s tough-guy portrayer Dennis
29 Gandalf the ___
30 Drinking to excess
31 Brought up incessantly
32 Aeschylus trilogy
33 "This Week at War" airer
34 Mineral found in igneous rocks
36 Took a mulligan on
38 Typical lab rat, e.g.
39 Circumferences
40 Yardbird
41 Cylindrical vessel with a flat bottom
42 Compounds found in wine
45 Ancient Mycenaean stronghold

by Patrick Berry

46 Do without
48 Pointed, in
   a way
49 Stymie

93 HARD

ACROSS

1 It operates under a royal charter
7 1996 movie starring Michael Jordan
15 Swank in Hollywood
16 Popular mixer
17 Low 90s, say
18 "I get your point!"
19 Many a first-time voter in 1920
20 Hilarious
21 Bald person's envy, maybe
22 "Imperialism, the Highest Stage of Capitalism" writer
23 Born yesterday
25 Balrog slayer, in fiction
30 Errs
32 Case worker's org.?
34 Stand for something
35 Grind
36 Expert with computers
39 Kudzu, e.g.
40 Per ___
42 With 49-Across, figure skating practice
43 Well-being
44 Novelty shop purchase
47 Dish often served with soy sauce or miso
49 See 42-Across
51 Neighborhood vandalism ammo
53 Super item?
57 Hardly close-mouthed
59 It breaks the "I before E" rule
60 Lack of vitality
61 Many a role in the Jason Bourne films
62 Frank
63 Brandy brand
64 Pigpens

DOWN

1 Springtime period
2 Stadium shout-out
3 M.V.P. of Super Bowls XLII and XLVI
4 U.C. Santa Cruz athlete
5 It borders the South China Sea
6 Young and others
7 Movie component
8 Contacting via Facebook, in a way
9 Whistling thorn, e.g.
10 Ingredient in Buffalo wings
11 Bionomics: Abbr.
12 Part of a routine
13 Interjection that comes from the Latin for "weary"
14 Billy famous for infomercials
20 Rite of passage participant, often
24 Industrial container
26 "A Heartbreaking Work of Staggering Genius" author
27 Quadrennial sporting event
28 See-through object
29 Fugitate
30 Buck
31 Liberal arts college 20 minutes north of Manhattan
33 Charade
37 Merry-go-round fixture, to a tot
38 ___ high (about that tall)
41 Sales rep's reimbursement, maybe
45 Big list maker
46 "The Lion Sleeps Tonight" hitmakers, with "the"
48 Bowser in the Super Mario series, e.g.
50 Inconsequential
52 10-Down, e.g.
53 Physicist Ernst who studied shock waves
54 "___ told often enough . . ."

by Joel Fagliano

55 Range
56 Common conjunction
58 Chow
60 Nelson, e.g.: Abbr.

ACROSS

1 High clouds?
9 Ancient pentathlon event
15 Approximately .264 gallons
16 Div. created in 1969
17 It gets the word out
18 New Valentine's phrase added on Sweethearts candy in 2010
19 Prince Edward I. clock setting
20 Having an underwhelmed response
22 Essence
23 Thought after an after-afterthought: Abbr.
25 Freshen
27 Scramble
28 Hot
30 War cry of the '60s
32 Smooth
34 "The Da Vinci Code" albino
35 "Brokeback Mountain" director
36 Hot dog's relative
38 Cable inits.
39 ___ tree
42 "Alas!"
44 Flavor
46 Hands-in-the-air phrase
50 McCarthy cohort
51 Big name in educational funding
52 Spread
54 Birds of prey
55 Etiolates
57 Incipience
59 Grp. involved in the Abbottabad raid
60 Onomatopoeic game on "The Price Is Right"
62 Time near the end of a time range
64 It might have a crust
65 Sophocles tribute that begins "Numberless are the world's wonders . . ."
66 Language of the Afghan national anthem
67 Cry from an arriving group

DOWN

1 Medicate oneself, say
2 Rampaging
3 Check that's inked, perhaps
4 Sharp
5 Spray
6 Fur source
7 Fish of sufficient size
8 Fur sources
9 Slangy pronoun
10 They're near appendices
11 Stock in an adult store
12 Name-brand targets?
13 Words below an eagle
14 A biochemical solid
21 Dock, in a way
24 Itinerary abbr.
26 Spring locales
29 Character
31 Spikes
33 Spring locales
37 1997 Nielsen title role
39 Common admission requirement
40 Actor who might grin and bare it?
41 Director's cutoff
42 Chorus member?
43 Secrecy, with "the"
45 Game show purchase
46 Rare dynamic marking seen in Tchaikovsky's Sixth Symphony
47 Objects from everyday life
48 United group
49 "In order to know virtue, we must first acquaint ourselves with vice" speaker
53 Hold off
56 Sketch

by David Quarfoot

58 Department head?
61 Conceptual art
pioneer
63 Line from Homer

ACROSS

1 Aunties' sisters
7 Gold medal
15 Fly
16 Prepare to take off, perhaps
17 Evers of civil rights
18 Quick seasonal greeting?
19 Ice cream gobbler's woe
21 A.L. East team, on scoreboards
22 Ear-relevant
23 Old Norse work
24 Orange exterior
25 United entities before 1991: Abbr.
26 "Get Smart" enemy agency
27 2008 Israeli political biography
28 Beater of a full boat in poker
30 Naturally bright
31 Develops
34 C6H6
35 Stilted-sounding "Consider it done"
36 "The Godfather" enforcer who "sleeps with the fishes"
37 "Cheers" alternative, in a letter
38 Providers of inside looks?

39 "Minnie the Moocher" feature
43 Archer of film
44 In a day, say
45 Solving aid
46 End of a line in England
47 Hit MTV series starting in 2009
50 Double grace period?
52 Start operating, datewise
53 Vronsky's love
54 Stoolies, often
55 Like clams during winter
56 1993 rap hit in which Snoop Doggy Dogg popularized the term "bootylicious"

DOWN

1 Relatives of merengues
2 Heads off
3 Where trapeze artists connect
4 Ancient talisman with mathematical properties
5 ___ advantage
6 One bound to do work
7 Ball wear
8 Popping Prozacs, perhaps

9 Common statue setting
10 Ask
11 Legendary raptor
12 Figure skater Brasseur
13 Directed attention (on)
14 Runs over
20 Goes over
24 Source of false returns
26 Film critic Pauline
27 Magazine articles
29 E-tailing specifications
30 They can get choppy
31 "Ponyo" writer/director Hayao ___
32 In unison
33 Booms
34 Pickle
36 Pierce with lines
38 "West Side Story" Oscar winner
40 Like the I.B.M. PC, often
41 Light show?
42 Minute
44 Four enter them, but only two survive
47 Tennis star Novotna
48 Over there, to bards
49 Practice with gloves on
51 Once known as

by Steven Riley

ACROSS

1 Stage Deli staple
12 Gas ending
15 Writer who held 14 honorary doctorates
16 Deliver hooks, e.g.
17 Stephen King's next novel after "Christine"
18 Many a cell product
19 Quito-to-Lima dir.
20 Bolted
21 Melodic passages
23 Bottom part
24 Oyster Bay hamlet
25 "Hammerklavier," for one
28 Is in the can
29 Singer of the 2011 #1 hit "Someone Like You"
30 Ranee's wear
31 Dreadlocks cover
32 NC-17, maybe
33 Grooved ring on many a ring
34 It may be open at a comedy club
35 Sound that a muzzle muffles
36 One active in the heat?
37 Black scavenger
38 They can answer the question "Who's your daddy?"
40 Jerboa's home
41 Origins
42 Volstead Act opponents
43 Throws together
44 Two-wheeled carriage
45 Away's partner
48 Accent reduction may be part of it: Abbr.
49 Great work
52 Computer add-on?
53 1951 Tony winner for "Call Me Madam"
54 The idiot brother in "Our Idiot Brother"
55 It borders the Land of Lincoln

DOWN

1 Disco swingers?
2 Plural suffix for conditions
3 Turner Prize institution
4 Part of une danse
5 Collectible record
6 Chutney-dipped appetizer
7 Pre-Soviet succession
8 One may provide passage
9 Health care grp.
10 Crevice-lurking predator
11 1957 hit for Perry Como
12 Like some blood
13 One passed out on New Year's Eve
14 What many fans generate
22 Ending for 23-Across
23 Having nothing to part with?
24 More likely to go off
25 Choice for a bed made in the kitchen
26 ___ Line (German/Polish border)
27 Novel
28 Staggers
30 Mennonites and others
33 Diamond lane
34 Gravitation consideration
36 They have job listings
37 Does over, as a document
39 French pronoun
40 Hand wringer's words
42 Overpower
44 Be unsettled
45 Damage control grp.
46 "Ev'rybody Wants to Be ___" (Disney film tune)

by Barry C. Silk

47 Novelist Bazin
50 "___ nuff!"
51 N.Y.C. commuting
  debut of 1904

ACROSS

1 Pet subject
9 Presents itself
15 "My pleasure"
17 Dubious claim after crying wolf
18 They may be carted around
19 Defense option
20 Enough, to Étienne
22 Grammar subject
23 Guam-to-Tahiti dir.
25 Common canal locale: Abbr.
29 Great red spot?
37 Unlikely place to take one's business
38 Promise, e.g.
39 Weeps and wails
40 Old English letters
41 "The Black Cat" writer's inits.
42 "Yesterday," e.g.
47 Really tick off
52 Funny
55 Let go to pot?
56 1991 Jackie Chan film
60 Sign words often accompanied by an airplane symbol
61 Megillah book
62 One may get printed

DOWN

1 One of the Pointer Sisters
2 Some vaults
3 They're in the first draft
4 Kind of porridge
5 With 54-Down, kind of store
6 First name in 1970s tyranny
7 Giant among Giants
8 Words before problem or department
9 Drop ___ (be suggestive)
10 Dreaded believer?
11 Put under the table
12 Not peruse
13 Actress Watson
14 Admitted to a doctor's office
16 More or less follower
21 Mrs. F. Scott Fitzgerald and others
22 Like many monograms on clothing
24 Arrange for
26 Rather colloquial?
27 Much paper, originally
28 Compassion
29 33-Down, for one
30 Formed another congress

31 N.B.A. great Thomas
32 Pirates' hangout
33 Plains people
34 Like many bagged vegetables
35 Part of a Flintstone's yell
36 Consumes impolitely
43 Winged
44 Gas unit
45 Pirates' hangout
46 Starbucks has one
48 Gas units
49 Get a divorce
50 Make right
51 Sign of a narrowing path
52 John Paul II, e.g.
53 "Beowulf" or "Gilgamesh"
54 See 5-Down
57 "Tell Me More" broadcaster
58 Runner with a hood
59 Valuable stuff in a pocket

by Joe Krozel

ACROSS

1 Makeup of some insulating sheets
5 Vulcans and others
15 Sixth-day creation
16 Singer with a black V-shaped collar
17 Food product for the eco-conscious
19 "That man" in "I'm Gonna Wash That Man Right Outa My Hair"
20 It's often shown with hands
21 Word for a keeper?
22 Hands off
24 Approx. camera flash duration
26 Ending with plural, in Plymouth
27 Words before before
28 South Vietnam's ___ Dinh Diem
30 "Ooh-la-la!"
32 Across, in odes
33 Seize, old-style
35 Wine shop offering, informally
36 "The Girl I Knew Somewhere" group, with "the"
38 "My Best Friend's Girl" group
42 Harboring cold feelings?

43 It's often in the spotlight
45 Left-arrow abbr.
46 Language that gave us "catamaran"
48 Spotted à la Tweety Bird
49 Family
50 Gerrymander
51 Like many a teen idol
53 Ray with lines
55 National competitor
57 Selling point
59 Cloudless, in Saint-Cloud
60 Features of some Amerindian embroidery
63 Put in the spotlight
64 They have balls
65 Put through a chop shop, say
66 Brand name used by Jersey Standard

DOWN

1 Moved over, say
2 1781 Mozart premiere
3 Demographic lauded in a 1965 song
4 Not so scanty
5 Introspective query
6 Carnival follower

7 Hugo-winning 1994 memoir
8 Wheels from the Netherlands
9 Pleasing bank statement?
10 "Self-Reliance" essayist's inits.
11 Plane figs.
12 Fables, often
13 Knighted diamond magnate Oppenheimer
14 Spin out on the ice?
18 "___ Twelve Men" (Greer Garson film)
23 Old dagger
25 Trick
29 Beano alternative
31 Minute Maid brand
33 Holdover
34 "Vulcan's chimney"
37 Cityhopper carrier
39 Laugh hard
40 Geckos, e.g.
41 Guarantees
44 Not bound by 20-Across
46 Temple of Vesta locale
47 Group indiscriminately
49 Certain toast
50 ___-fire
52 Dirty
54 Defib setting
56 Dirty film

by Scott Atkinson

58 Where le nez is
61 She played Cécile in "Dangerous Liaisons"
62 Ending letters

ACROSS

1 Letter carrier
8 Quaint place to live?
13 Extreme choice
16 Farmer's enemy
17 Much-favored person
18 Some subatomic particles
19 Retired
20 ___ Plus (razor brand)
22 Home to a school of pre-Socratic philosophers
23 Comedic duo?
24 Using an Rx, say
26 Ron who played Tarzan
27 Where your ship may come in
28 Loafs on the job
30 Filling point
34 "When I was a lad . . ."
36 Smooth
37 Six-time Tony winner of 1984
40 Stump the crowd?
41 Vet employer, maybe: Abbr.
42 16-Across, e.g.
43 Rambled
45 Bygone
46 86 or 99 on "Get Smart": Abbr.
47 Tangles
49 Chip in a dish, e.g.

53 Gush (over)
55 Round nos.
56 It's often backed up
57 Foreign assistance org. since 1961
59 Use advantageously, as an idea
61 Big name in watches
62 Place to find subs
63 Rob of "Melrose Place"
64 Discharged

DOWN

1 Word with square or number
2 Helpless?
3 "Can you beat that?!"
4 Bonanzas
5 Raised
6 Rule among true crime writers
7 Run wild
8 Physical "Psst!"
9 Grandnephew in 1960s TV
10 Not marked up
11 Cat's gift
12 Final words?
14 Passing remark?
15 "Gentle reader, may you never feel what I then felt!" speaker
21 Attach (to)
24 Instrument with a bell

25 Average
29 [This is scary!]
30 Lose it
31 Contents of the rightmost column of a table
32 Words of anticipation
33 Political writer ___ Bai
35 Scoop
38 Prizm and Spectrum, once
39 They're not hot for very long
44 Anchorage-to-Fairbanks dir.
48 Order: Abbr.
49 Contents of many outtakes
50 Wash against gently
51 Win by ___
52 Declined
54 Figure on the front of Olympic medals since 1928
56 Forward who wore #10
58 Elements of some lists
60 Quickly turn back

by Mike Nothnagel

ACROSS

1 Many a museum dinosaur display
8 Suited to the stage
15 What a telemarketer often hears before a click
17 Reward in the offing?
18 Three in a match, maybe
19 Covent Garden area
20 Taking some doing
23 Stains
27 Bleed (for)
31 Probably will
32 Back 40?
34 Nonstarter's lack
36 Threaten collapse
37 The Cherokee deemed it good training for war
38 Masters
39 Like Bacharach/David songs
40 Checked the meter?
42 Provider of up-to-the-minute info?
45 Follower of blood and guts
49 Might just
53 Scottie
54 Homemakers out on a limb?
55 Site of the first British colony in the Caribbean, 1624

DOWN

1 Leap-the-___ (world's oldest operating roller coaster)
2 Hungary's ___ Nagy
3 Doing the job
4 Huge-taloned menaces
5 Put down
6 Parmesan pronoun
7 Name meaning "grace"
8 Heroic son of Prince Anchises
9 Mustard family member
10 Easily snapping
11 He got a tennis scholarship from U.C.L.A.
12 Old bomber
13 Fat part
14 Reds great Roush
16 Traitors' Gate locale
20 Present
21 Senior
22 1930s film dog
23 Mandates
24 "___ signo vinces" (Constantine I's motto)
25 29-Down, for one
26 Two are often put in
27 "My Fair Lady" setting
28 Where to feel the beat?
29 Its capital is Wiesbaden
30 European city whose name sounds like two letters of the alphabet
32 Shameful gain
33 Nose-burning
35 Like much lumber
39 "The Last of the Mohicans" craft
40 Strawberry is one
41 One engaged in bucket-making
42 Toots
43 St. ___, Cornwall
44 Frobe who played Goldfinger
45 Sign letters on the cross
46 Execute a 47-Down, e.g.
47 See 46-Down
48 Rocky outcrops
49 China's ___ dynasty
50 Affliction a k a "blue devils"
51 Strawberry was one
52 Chafe

by Robert H. Wolfe

ACROSS

1 "I'd like to hear any justification at all"
16 Young and inexperienced
17 "Yeah, and . . . ?"
18 Olympians brought them down
19 Flutter the eyelids, say
20 First name in horror
21 "I should ___ die with pity": King Lear
24 Surfing business?
27 Hole in the wall
30 "Roxana: The Fortunate Mistress" novelist
31 Antebellum Ohio, e.g.
34 Like much lumber
35 Intl. group whose biennial conferences are focuses of protest
36 Follower of grazing cattle
38 Put away
39 Word repeated before "lama sabachthani" in Mark 15
41 Frames wind up on them
43 Some crosses
45 "Love Actually" co-star, 2003

46 River that the dead drank from, in myth
47 You may leave them in stitches: Abbr.
48 "Das ___ gut!"
51 Bottom
53 Convertible
56 Bar cliché
61 It shows many flight numbers
62 Doesn't take the cake?

DOWN

1 You'll get it from CliffsNotes
2 Way to fry
3 Promise one will
4 Better
5 With 35-Down, have no malice
6 Quoted figs.
7 Sweet ending?
8 Big inits. in paperback publishing
9 Urban rumblers
10 Pulitzer-winning poet Armantrout and others
11 Ready for publication
12 What Web page sponsors may link to
13 Seat of Marin County, Calif.
14 "Listen up!" to Luis
15 State bordering the Pacific: Abbr.

21 Tangle up
22 One who shouldn't be helping
23 Winner of over 100 Pulitzer Prizes, briefly
25 Chiwere speakers
26 Time to abstain
28 Things done for fun, for short
29 From
31 Home of the U.S. Army Women's Museum
32 Upper house support
33 Misunderstands, say
35 See 5-Down
37 ___ volente
40 "Ow-w-w!"
42 They're hard to figure out
44 Always, in scores
49 "Rotten School" series author
50 Photographer's bath
52 Underscore neighbor
53 Mindless
54 Some MoMA works
55 Hide
56 Small bark
57 ___ good day
58 "Odi et ___": Catullus
59 2000s, e.g.: Abbr.
60 One may be tight

by Tim Croce

ACROSS

1 Skirt raisers?
9 Toward the tip
15 Equivalent of "ibidem"
16 ___ 400 (Pennsylvania Nascar event)
17 They're often swiped at stores
18 Parnassian
19 Stereotypical bouncers
20 Do some post-harvesting work
21 Marion ___, Emmy-winning actress on "Bewitched"
22 A hand
24 Singer in the "Odyssey"
25 "What ___?
26 Subject for Enrico Caruso
28 Kiss hit "Rock and Roll All ___"
29 Western wear
31 Cousin of bridge
35 Discards
36 2001 presidential biography by Edmund Morris
40 Pull down
41 Michael who sang "I'm a lumberjack and I'm O.K."

42 Rudimentary run
46 Puts on a graph, say
48 Zero-deg. setting
49 Source of a feather in one's cap?
50 Symbol of power
52 TV hotline
54 Captured for posterity, maybe
55 Spanish port
56 Classic Lorre role
57 Jabbed back
58 Like classic stories
59 Macramé creators

DOWN

1 Helpful
2 Lorry supply
3 Shows reservations
4 Molière contemporary
5 Put to shame
6 "Heads up!"
7 Many an HBO show
8 Shrink time, say
9 8-Down, e.g.: Abbr.
10 Some toy bears, informally
11 They have two goals
12 Sets of friends
13 Liqueur sweetened with syrup
14 Locale in a much-studied 1934 photo
23 1970s–80s N.B.A. nickname

26 Classical subject of a Velázquez painting in the Prado
27 Gone from a plate
29 "The Beverly Hillbillies" role
30 1920 Democratic presidential nominee
31 "Make a searching and fearless moral inventory of ourselves," in Alcoholics Anonymous
32 Digital bone
33 1980s–90s Ford model
34 "Whatever"
37 Catchy tune
38 Medicinal tea source
39 Narcolepsy drug
42 Totally shaken
43 Family name in English literature
44 See 49-Down
45 Strong mounts
47 Walls of the heart
49 With 44-Down, it had its grand opening on 10/1/1982
51 Ranked player
53 ___ the hat

by Mark Diehl

ACROSS

1 One with a famous opening act?
8 Invite out for
13 They get the scoop at work
16 Run
17 Trying to win a radio contest, say
18 Figure in a doctor's office
19 Light breakfast
20 Liberal opening?
22 Notes come out of them
23 Old game co. that made D&D
24 Tree with catkins
26 Temporary retirements?
27 Intrepidity
29 "The Sorrows of Young Werther" author
31 Runs out of energy
33 Fix up
35 "Holy cow!"
36 Frustratingly difficult
39 Suffix with Caesar
40 Excrete
41 Swing wildly
42 11-Down, usually
44 Argument
46 Part of the intro to a piece of "Champagne Music"
47 Area in front of a basketball net, informally
49 ___-bear
52 Allocation of some pork spending?
53 A.L. East squad, on scoreboards
54 Quickly mount
57 Bit of funny business
59 Fools around
61 Advertiser with a computer-generated mascot
62 Game that gave rise to the expression "ace in the hole"
63 Thomas Cromwell's earldom
64 Positive or negative

DOWN

1 Fred has one in "Scooby-Doo" cartoons
2 Assistance for short people?
3 Thumb twiddler
4 Roll in a field
5 Do ___ (celebrate, sort of)
6 Player losing to the 49ers in Super Bowl XVI or XXIII
7 Intl. soccer powerhouse
8 Original airer of "The Jetsons"
9 ___ Crosley, author of the 2008 best seller "I Was Told There'd Be Cake"
10 Held back
11 Item in a trophy case
12 Cross-country trips, perhaps
14 Soul mate
15 N.F.L. All-Pro player Chris
21 What a fugue may be written for
25 "Passage to Marseille" actor, 1944
27 Valve opening?
28 Some flakes
30 Specialty doc
31 Connection indicators
32 "You're telling me!"
34 Discover, as a solution
36 21, often
37 2011 revolution locale
38 Item in a tent, maybe
43 "Ooh-la-la!"
45 "Better than nothing"
48 Informal approvals
49 Shoot up
50 "Breezing Up (A Fair Wind)" artist, 1876
51 When to celebrate el Día de los Reyes
55 "Outside the Lines" airer
56 Comprehensive
58 Boat navigator, informally

by Mike Nothnagel

60 "___ Yu" (collection
also known as "The
Analects of
Confucius")

ACROSS

1 Pettifog
9 Home of Texas A&M International University
15 Reprimander of Miss Gulch
16 Flew united?
17 Not covered anywhere
19 One in a powerful house
20 "Cats" Tony winner Trevor
21 Pop sharer
22 Legions
23 Heartless sort
25 Like many suites
26 Reason for a replay
27 "Join me?"
28 Prefix with -matic
29 Nautilus shell liners
30 "All Day Strong. All Day Long" sloganeer
31 Pole dance?
34 Their scales aid in location
36 "Do ___?"
37 Remove with leverage
39 Grp. on the floor
40 The health-conscious often take them
41 Bug about bills
44 Olden dagger
45 Uncommon delivery
46 Manager, briefly
47 Finishing touch on a diamond?
48 Dermatologist's concern
49 Affects radically
51 Events marked by large streamers
54 Was a real stinker
55 Pass
56 Meetings kept under wraps
57 Utterly unpredictable

DOWN

1 It's barely about a foot
2 Deliverer of the 1992 "Murphy Brown speech"
3 Relax during a massage, as a muscle
4 Bothered
5 Offers for lots
6 Drive away
7 Brown with the Band of Renown
8 Spring
9 Bit of rough housing
10 Kirk who played the first big-screen Superman
11 Mug, say
12 Program developments
13 Like raspberries
14 They're unmatched in footwear
18 "Hey, it's something to consider"
24 Transport
25 Bed for some kebabs
27 Tin finish?
29 Worker with vital information?
30 Film composer Clausen and others
31 Get off on the wrong foot
32 Erhard succeeded him in 1963
33 "The Vanishing American" novelist, 1925
35 Taking great pains
38 Shower surprise
40 Some quiet riots
41 "André" playwright William
42 1982 and 1991 Pulitzer winner for fiction
43 Ford's press secretary
46 Defense grp. formed in 1954
48 Four-time Gold Glove Award winner Boone
50 Man in la famille
52 Agreements
53 Duct lead-in

by Barry C. Silk

ACROSS

1 One called upon to decide
5 Back cover?
10 Keep the complaints coming
14 Pavlova of the ballet
15 Head stone?
16 Nondairy alternative
17 O.K.
20 First #1 hit for the Commodores
21 Counterfeit
22 Horse shows?
23 Hard to see through, say
24 Laid eyes on
25 Hardly seaworthy
26 Takes shape
27 Apple seed
30 About
31 One of Franklin's certainties
32 Little Tramp prop
33 Diagnosis deliverers: Abbr.
34 Expended some nervous energy
35 Commuting option in Georgia's capital
36 Jockey's uniform
37 First female chancellor of Germany
38 Attributes (to), with "up"

40 Former "CBS Morning News" co-anchor Bill
41 Spotlight
44 "Yeah, right!"
45 Play money?
46 The Donald's second ex
47 Small letter
48 Some ruminants
49 Bob ___, "To Kill a Mockingbird" villain
50 Santa ___ Valley (winegrowing region)

DOWN

1 Play group
2 Getting better
3 Not caught up
4 First son, sometimes
5 Warp drive repairman on the original "Star Trek"
6 Koran memorizer
7 Koran reciter
8 Like a town that used to be a ghost town
9 Schooner features
10 Sat on a sill, maybe
11 Finnish architect Aalto
12 Tries out for a part
13 Part of many a tech school's name

18 "The North Pole" author, 1910
19 Phone company offers
23 Hardly stocky
24 "The Battle of the ___" (D.W. Griffith film)
26 Pick-up sticks piece
27 English physician James who gave his name to a disease
28 Not ready to go, you might say
29 Ring
31 "I want the lowdown!"
32 Not drawn true to life
34 Starchy dish
35 Good reason for promotion
36 "Tom ___, Detective" (1896 novel)
37 Held in common
38 Part of a boomtown's skyline
39 Cause of careless mistakes
40 Rise
41 Utterly exhausted
42 Literary governess's surname
43 Courtroom cry

by Patrick Berry

ACROSS

1 Stuff between some cake layers
16 Brood terribly
17 They may perform minor surgeries
18 Menu general
19 Harbors
20 Jobs announcement?
21 Refreshment site
24 Thing that's picked
26 Old-time actresses Allgood and Haden
30 Ad ___
32 Tom Sawyer's half brother
34 Org. with lead concerns
35 Staff member checking the books
41 Self-correcting or self-cleaning, say
42 Put some matter in the gray matter?
43 "Nasty!"
44 Kill
45 Besides
46 Big pictures
49 Ball-bearing piece
51 Sycosis source, informally
55 Trucial States, today: Abbr.
57 Buzzsaw Brown, e.g.
59 Little Parisian?
60 Ruthless

66 Something baffling
67 Creates more incentive to win

DOWN

1 Poem comprised of quotations
2 Common language in Niger
3 Others, to Juan
4 Calculator button
5 In dire need of gas
6 First name in Polish politics
7 Literary lion
8 1955 sci-fi film that was one of the first to use Technicolor
9 Contracted time period?
10 More than mar
11 Killers that may go through hoops
12 City near Oneida Lake
13 ". . . ___ fool returneth to his folly": Proverbs 26:11
14 Thing to fry in
15 8-Down characters, briefly
22 She pounded the East Coast in 2011
23 Alternative to Tempur-Pedic

25 Luis in the Red Sox Hall of Fame
27 Like many things that come back
28 "Every man will be ___ if he can": Thoreau
29 South Asian wear: Var.
31 Moon of Jupiter
33 Ticket, informally
35 Color-streaked playing marble
36 Grp. involved with Brown v. Board of Education
37 McAloo ___ (burger at McDonald's in India)
38 About
39 Apollo's birthplace
40 Otherwise
47 Round dance officials
48 Hall-of-Fame jockey Earl
50 Olympic-level
52 Vertical, at sea
53 Nez ___
54 Ear protectors
56 Time to evolve?
58 Those, to Juan
60 Seagoing sort
61 Cry upon figuring out 66-Across
62 Trombonist Winding
63 Express

by Gary J. Whitehead

64 Time of year for
much raking: Abbr.
65 Grp. with a piece
plan?

ACROSS

1 Goldeneye relative
5 Emergency extractor
15 "Must've been something ___"
16 No night owl
17 Jags of the 1960s and '70s
18 Eggbeater
19 Election extension?
20 Wrestling event
21 Only one of the 13 Colonies not touching the Atl. Ocean
22 Go crazy
24 Board provision
26 They're prepared to sell snake oil
27 Stock keeper
28 Third qtr. closer
31 See
32 Ferris wheel in Dallas that is the tallest in North America
34 Angle in botany
35 Support
36 El ___
37 Very turbulent situation
39 Slopes
40 Lifesaving squad: Abbr.
41 Wrong
42 Collector of dust bunnies
43 ESPN anchor Kolber
44 Word before and after "for"
45 Moolah
48 Ancient neighbor of Judah
49 Bladder
50 Follower of "Help!"
53 Feature of some lenses
54 ___ Line (international boundary)
55 Alfredo sauce brand
56 One concerned with bouquets
57 Buzz producers

DOWN

1 Wells Fargo Center event, informally
2 38-Down's second chance
3 They never end
4 Jazzman Montgomery
5 The Pink Panther and others
6 Showed delight, in a way
7 Certiorari, e.g.
8 Olympus OM-1, e.g.
9 Olive ___
10 Browning equipment
11 Smearing in ink?
12 "The fix ___"
13 Shedder of spores
14 Mother of the Valkyries
20 Three-time All-Star pitcher Pappas
23 "Mack the Knife" composer
24 Annual "Hot 100" publisher
25 They're historically significant
27 Generated
28 Cardinal for 22 years
29 Newark suburb
30 Security account?
32 Robe material
33 Fixes at an animal hospital
35 Complete
38 Person making a mark
39 Grouch
42 Crack investigator's target?
43 Buffalo pro
44 Quiet type
45 It's often knitted
46 Designer Gernreich
47 "___ Holden" (Irving Bacheller novel)
48 Very
51 "Still Crazy" star, 1998
52 Family nickname
53 Singsong syllable

by Barry C. Silk

ACROSS

1 Fault line?
8 Rope holding down a bowsprit
15 Great part for Duvall?
16 1945 Tommy Dorsey hit
17 Medium frequencies include them
18 Journalists James and James Jr.
19 Nigerian language
20 Ingredient in gourmet potato chips
22 ___ de guerre
23 Scary sucker, for short
25 Bastes
26 Look down
27 Shot stuff
29 LP insert?
30 Pungent fish topper
31 Longtime ace
33 Goes gray
35 Part of some fruit drink names
37 Film with the protagonist "Z"
38 Any of three title characters in a long-running Cartoon Network series
42 See 46-Across
46 With 42-Across, old ad mascot who sang "It's dandy for your teeth"
47 Worked (up)
49 Source of the word "robot"
50 Salad, often
51 ___ up (brawl)
53 Big name in jewelry retail
54 Mouths, to Marius
55 Spartan
57 Ad trailer?
58 Reaches the age of
60 It forms much of Lombardy's southern border
62 One
63 Central feature of St. Peter's Square
64 Taco alternative
65 "Coppelia" composer

DOWN

1 Parent's peremptory "reason"
2 Common barn roof
3 Passenger's status
4 Taxonomy suffix
5 Drum and bass parts
6 Through
7 Get heat from?
8 Part of French Polynesia
9 Some German models
10 Boom follower, maybe
11 Boom maker, once
12 Gnarly
13 Author of "The Stranger Beside Me," 1980
14 Beatles tune that begins "If you wear red tonight"
21 Like arias
24 Sugar
26 Dash
28 Oscar winner after "On the Waterfront"
30 Onetime Lake Texcoco dweller
32 Papuan port
34 Having five sharps
36 Drink that had a Wild Red variety
38 Drink that has a Ruby Red variety
39 Philippine province on Luzon
40 The Aggies of the Big West Conf.
41 "What ___?"
43 Steak or chop choice
44 Cover-up witnessed by millions?
45 Relatives of dik-diks
48 Car bar
51 So as not to be overheard, say
52 Alabama or Missouri
55 ___-Pacific
56 First name in long jumping

by Ned White

59 Small creature that undergoes metamorphosis

61 Clinton or Bush, once

ACROSS

1 Drive-in theater, in old slang
11 Klutzes
15 Like some freely available software
16 Streaming video giant
17 What an up-and-coming band wants to snag
18 Keatsian or Horatian
19 Say "Ta-da!," say
20 "Hmm . . ."
22 "___ Maria"
24 PC file extension
25 The shakes, for short
26 Together
31 Cary of "The Princess Bride"
33 They might be cut at a salon
34 Kind of rock or candy
36 Not fancy at all
38 Bob Hope, for 18 Oscar ceremonies
39 When repeated, response to "Who wants ice cream?"
40 Traffic cone
41 Fidgeting during a poker game, e.g.
42 Grind
43 Dastard
44 Jai alai basket
46 Produces new music for, as a movie

48 Shake
49 Company name ender
51 Where Barry Bonds was an All-American, in brief
52 First female dean of Harvard Law School
56 Football Hall-of-Famer Marchetti
60 Michigan college
61 Craft in a "Star Wars" battle scene
63 Like some German nouns: Abbr.
64 Individually
65 Language from which "hubbub" comes
66 "The Case of the Demure Defendant" protagonist

DOWN

1 Offering from a Parisian butcher
2 Copycat
3 Like some Spanish wine
4 What people waving their arms might produce
5 It has more museums per capita than any other country: Abbr.
6 Lots
7 Fully exposed
8 Ready, in Rouen
9 Caesarean section?

10 Wired, in a way
11 Eager pupil's cry
12 Where to see some German models
13 Rubble neighbor
14 Is god-awful
21 ___ Avivian
23 Gripper
26 Scoffing comment
27 One hurling insults
28 Fictional narrator of "Legends of the Old Plantation"
29 Home to the Browns and the Reds
30 Bottom
32 Moe Howard catchphrase
35 Moe Howard, for Chris Diamantopoulos, in 2012
37 Tips
40 Ranks for jarheads: Abbr.
42 Sleeveless option
45 ___ Maria
47 Levelheadedness
48 ___ Dixon, self-styled seer who wrote an astrology book for dogs
50 "The Dark Knight" actor
53 "Great" detective of kiddie lit
54 Will of "The Waltons"
55 Way off

by Natan Last

57 "Really?"
58 Literary captain who says "I am not what you call a civilized man!"
59 ___ Ishii ("Kill Bill" character)
62 Group of whales

110 HARD

ACROSS

1 Drinking problem
9 If all goes swimmingly
15 Sugar
16 André and Mia adopted her
17 Change-producing agent
18 Water park recreation
19 Big dogs
20 1969 Tony winner for "Promises, Promises"
21 Colon's meaning, at times
22 When to see der Mond
23 Big name in gourmet chocolate
26 More likely to be bowdlerized
30 Chiwere speaker
31 Emmy-winning show of 2007, '08 and '09
35 Rom. tongue
36 Didn't demur
37 Face-topping figure
38 1955 Dior debut
40 Tiropita ingredient
41 Maximally mean
42 Nearly flawless bodies?
43 Place
46 1989 E.P.A. target
48 One in the closet
50 Starts to stagnate
54 Smallish printing format
55 Response to a surprising statement
56 One may be required to park
57 Start to squirm
58 2009–11 Republican National Committee chairman
59 Their voices really carry

DOWN

1 Fast shuffle
2 ___ Debevoise, Marilyn Monroe's "How to Marry a Millionaire" role
3 Some turnovers: Abbr.
4 It goes whichever way the wind blows
5 Apollo, for one
6 Sailor's behind
7 Piece offer?
8 Forest race of fantasy
9 Respecting
10 What seeds are often planted in
11 2008 Libertarian presidential candidate
12 Computing behemoth
13 Coordinate
14 Like best friends
23 Woman who "drank Champagne and danced all night," in song
24 Rom. tongue
25 Terse demurral
27 Posse, e.g.
28 Early radio receiver
29 Kin of -niks
31 Bits
32 Draft team
33 Reference
34 Rondos, e.g.
36 Big ray
39 Magic show?
40 Producer of the venom solenopsin
42 Annual George Jean ___ Award for Dramatic Criticism
43 Bazaar makeup
44 Indicator of silence
45 ___ Rios de Minas, Brazil
47 It might be a triple
49 Mechanical
50 Pen pals?
51 Quintillionth: Prefix
52 Locale in a Beatles title
53 Kikkoman options

1	2	3	4	5	6	7	8	■	9	10	11	12	13	14
15								■	16					
17								■	18					
19								■	20					
■	■	■	21				■	■	■	22				
23	24	25			■	26	27	28	29			■	■	■
30				■	31							32	33	34
35			■	36						■	37			
38			39						■	40				
■	■	■	41					■	42					
43	44	45			■	■	■	46	47			■	■	■
48					49	■	50					51	52	53
54						■	55							
56						■	57							
58						■	59							

by Caleb Madison

ACROSS

1 Ones pressed for cash, briefly
5 1997 #1 hit with a nonsense title
11 Many a bugger
14 See 63-Across
15 Code that's dangerous to break
16 Hermano de la madre
17 ___ en scène
18 More like a gymnast's body
19 Cartoon character who cries "You eediot!"
20 It may be acknowledged with a slap
23 Bad stroke
24 Back, in a way
25 Having the lead?
29 Real go-getter
30 Baker's dozen, maybe
33 Reading letters from the end?
34 TV's "hipster doofus"
37 Big name in footwear
39 Wish
40 Ticker with cachet
42 Watch it
47 Temporary

50 "9 to 5" director Higgins
51 Bad tool for a toddler to find
55 N.L. West team, on scoreboards
56 One seen in a shower
57 Ramirez of "Grey's Anatomy"
58 It's often illegal to hang one
59 Cry for more
60 2006–08 heavyweight champion Maskaev
61 Article in the Louvre?
62 High
63 With 14-Across, cruise bonus

DOWN

1 Tops
2 Wee bit
3 Fish out of water
4 Word chanted at a celebratory party
5 Routs, with "down"
6 When the Salt Lake City Olympics took place
7 Longtime first name in TV talk
8 Court paper showing one team's points
9 Comical Cheri
10 Adidas vis-à-vis Reebok

11 Alien
12 Like some navels
13 Jon Voight's New York birthplace
21 Air and water, e.g.
22 Yellow shade
26 Runaway
27 Organic compound
28 Scrappers put them up
31 Sprung thing
32 Response facilitator: Abbr.
34 What water lacks
35 When to get back to work, perhaps
36 Endpoint of pilgrims' progress?
37 Big name in frozen food
38 Circle
41 Snowboarders compete in them
43 Some Rodin pieces
44 Lye, for one
45 Like many grandstands
46 Tee off
48 Apropos of
49 Retail giant with the mascots Red Ruff and Blue Mews
52 Extra-bright
53 Bolted
54 He talked only to Wilbur

by Allan E. Parrish

ACROSS

1 One with a coat of many colors
10 Asian sea name
14 Girl group with a 1986 #1 hit
15 "Sì, mi chiamano ____" (Puccini aria)
16 Like telescopes
17 The Olympic Australis, e.g.
18 Unlocked?
19 1977 Paul Davis hit that spent 25 weeks in the Top 40
21 Negligible
22 Rubber
24 Old man
25 "____ Time," 1952 million-selling Eddie Fisher hit
26 Solitary places
27 ____ Humpalot, Austin Powers villain
29 Pro ____
30 City NNE of Toledo
31 Game in which players offer a few words
34 Swingers hit on them at parties
35 Manila airport name
36 Like hurricane weather
37 Punishment, metaphorically
38 Bill who composed "Gonna Fly Now"
39 Big trap
42 CBer's place
43 "Clamshell" computers of old
45 Kennedy Center happening
46 First, second and third
48 Historic D.C. theater
49 Beast fought by Heracles
50 Donning, as loafers
53 Gloom
54 Chilling
55 Short winter day?
56 They may be heard in a temple

DOWN

1 Redeem
2 Second Triumvirate member
3 David with a role for himself on TV
4 Muscle ____
5 Junk
6 California's Montaña de ____ State Park
7 Duchess of Cornwall
8 Mates
9 Dishes eaten with the hands
10 Topic for Catullus
11 Shred
12 Rain forest region
13 Resting spots by the water
14 "Stop!" overseas
20 Pasta go-with
22 Four-time Oscar nominee (never a winner) in the 1930s
23 Motivators
26 Doesn't merely observe
28 Heady time for soldiers
29 Rapid turnover
30 They're hard to see through
31 Organization of Afro-American Unity founder
32 School house?
33 Comic strip that Chic Young abandoned to create "Blondie"
34 No-goodnik
36 Touching bottom?
38 Pet peeve?
39 Herbert Henry Asquith's socialite wife
40 ____ Snow, Russell Brand's character in "Forgetting Sarah Marshall" and "Get Him to the Greek"
41 "____ That a Time?" (Weavers album)
44 Poet credited with popularizing haiku
45 They may be heard in a temple
47 Signs

by Patrick Berry

48 Done, in Dunkirk
51 Wanamaker Trophy
   org.
52 Jewelry box item

ACROSS
1 Finery
8 Key for someone with 20/20 vision?
14 Audit targets
15 Concluding syllables
16 Take at an opportune time
17 Grooms
18 Modern chemistry experiment?
20 End of a dictionary
21 "The Scarperer" author
22 "Ciao"
24 "The cautious seldom ___": Confucius
25 Teary
27 ___ Fields
28 Winter ailment, informally
29 Get dressed for a party, say
31 52-Down unit
34 One who's blue, for short?
36 Poison ivy and others
37 Herb that causes euphoria
39 2022 World Cup host
41 Threshold
42 Raw
44 Lead character in Larry McMurtry's "Lonesome Dove"
47 Many a "Twilight" fan
49 Stick for a kite
50 Bankrupted
51 It might be covered by an umbrella
54 "Aladdin" princess
55 Remove spots from
56 Compass divisions
57 Most slapstick
58 Showcases of rock bands?
59 Ones who are hurting?

DOWN
1 Blow up, maybe
2 Fix for a wobbly table
3 Boot cover
4 Carving tools
5 A wolf may have one
6 Part of a jail cell
7 Prescription directive
8 Swept, say
9 Yards, e.g.
10 Command associated with numbers
11 "Couldn't agree with you more"
12 Seemed right
13 They go below signatures, briefly
15 Oct. 24
19 "Moby-Dick" setting
23 Lethal injection administerers
25 Hinged vessel, often
26 2001 British Open champion David
28 Britain's biggest-selling paper, with "The"
30 Certain board member: Abbr.
31 "Home Invasion" rapper
32 Avoid humiliation
33 Points in the direction of
35 First jazz musician to win a Pulitzer Prize
38 Raises
40 "Eugene Onegin" girl
43 Conditions, with "up"
44 Museum employees
45 Revolutionary state
46 Christmas tree base coverings
48 One who's really going places
50 Like the majority of Saudis
52 Informal pub
53 Brown green?
54 Prod

by Brendan Emmett Quigley

ACROSS

1 Accompanier of a thrown tomato
8 Reddish-orange gem
15 Settled
16 Like the sky
17 High-carb party snack
18 Midwest birthplace of Orson Welles and Don Ameche
19 Berry of "Mayberry R.F.D."
20 "Ha, see?!"
22 Heart, to Hadrian
23 Norway's Order of St. ___
25 Local protest acronym
26 Avoid work, in Britain
27 Try, informally
29 Jack-a-___ (hybrid dog)
30 Perfect Day maker
31 Green acres?
33 Basic bit of algebra
35 News newbie
36 Sartre's soul
37 Musée Rodin masterpiece
41 Home of the U.S. Army Airborne Forces
45 One of about a million on a jetliner
46 Fictional title sch. of a 1994 comedy film
48 Choice at some check-ins
49 "___ it!"
50 No-no for objectivity
52 Allowing no play
53 Adapted intro?
54 Make stylish
56 Bush much seen around Florida
57 Approach from out of nowhere
59 Stylish
61 Edible floppy disk?
62 Select from a menu
63 World's largest nocturnal primates
64 ___ Beer Night (1974 baseball promotion that ended in a riot)

DOWN

1 "I don't want to fight, man"
2 His opening line is "'Tis better as it is"
3 Like some markets and headphones
4 Bit of witchery
5 Brand with a paw print in its logo
6 Progeny
7 Advice from Dr. Ruth
8 Target of Fonzie's fist bumps
9 Impressionism?
10 One to walk with
11 Nigerian people
12 Pointless situation
13 Program guides
14 Talk of the town
21 Subj. in the 2007 documentary "Sicko"
24 Like some pullovers
26 Point out?
28 It might prevent a blackout
30 Friend of Pumbaa
32 "Are We There Yet?" airer
34 Skin pic?
37 Big name in weight-loss pills
38 Stowed
39 Prince of Darkness
40 Thin construction strips
41 Cool bit of trivia
42 For laughs
43 Like some fingernails and eyelashes
44 Bart Simpson catchphrase
47 Half-___
50 Rail nail
51 Tutu material
54 Make unbearable?
55 It may be unbearable
58 Andean tuber
60 Turn-of-the-century year

by Peter Wentz

ACROSS

1 Children's author Eleanor
6 Environment of many old PCs
11 Opposite of ample
13 Grapefruit taste-alike
14 Heated house for newborn chicks
16 Round number?
17 Restless, in scores
18 Go beyond seconds, say
19 Confirmation declaration
20 Some people in costume
21 "This doesn't exactly require a Ph.D."
23 What big banks underwent in 2009
24 ___ B (initial step)
25 They may be studied along with languages
33 What past performance may portend
35 Wild West symbol of authority
36 Practice at a track
38 Went for something else
39 SeaWorld attraction
40 Put people in their places?
41 Activity in "Ghostbusters"
42 Firewood measures
43 Attempt to recall the passed?
44 Stunned, in a way
45 German composer with a palindromic name

DOWN

1 Enclose in a recess
2 Eisenstein who directed "The Battleship Potemkin"
3 Some Asian believers
4 Hardly the self-effacing sort
5 Not so frantic
6 Really bothers
7 Give a smug look
8 Big name in diamonds
9 Last name in Chicago lore
10 It's unsettling to be out of them
12 Patch up, in a way, as a space shuttle
13 Quaint, dignified dance for couples
15 Valentine verse starter
16 Reach an agreement
22 Many a red dwarf
25 Things people "do" in the early afternoon
26 Mailbox checker's excited cry
27 Taught a lesson, maybe
28 Goes back on one's word?
29 Same old orders
30 Less congealed
31 Singer Morse with the 1952 hit "The Blacksmith Blues"
32 Giving expression to
33 Piñata-hitting occasion
34 Superlawyer Gerry who wrote "How to Argue and Win Every Time"
35 "___ no one"
37 "Old Time Rock & Roll" rocker

by Joe Krozel

ACROSS

1 Dessert for an infant
16 A straight shot it's not
17 "Bi-i-ig difference!"
18 Plea before going under
19 Him, in Hamburg
20 Certain chain unit: Abbr.
21 What's next to nothing in Nogales?
22 Paradise in literature
24 Produced some pitches
28 "Guten ___" (German greeting)
31 Beard growing out of an ear
32 San Francisco's ___ Valley
33 It may be pulled out while holding something up
38 Not so significantly
39 Cause for urgent action
40 Gothic leader?
41 Push around
42 Very conservative
43 [Don't touch my food!]
45 One chained to a desk, say
46 Certain chain units: Abbr.
47 Prefix with central
49 Going through
50 Fell
53 Tycoon who was the first person in New York City to own a car
59 Best seller that begins "Children are not rugged individualists"
60 Least accessible parts

DOWN

1 Eastern titles
2 Entirely, after "in"
3 Hodges who called baseball's "shot heard 'round the world"
4 Fay's "King Kong" role
5 "Absolutely!"
6 Taquería tidbit
7 Jet
8 Title in an order
9 Brand-new toy?
10 Net sales
11 Terminal list: Abbr.
12 Many stored hoses
13 Czech martyr Jan
14 Gen. Bradley's area: Abbr.
15 Person going into a house?: Abbr.
21 Man in a tree?
22 Liking a lot
23 Name shared by two U.S. presidents
25 Lets off the hook?
26 Unclaimed
27 Upper crust
28 Trouper's skill
29 New arrival of the 1950s?
30 More than fascinate
31 It shares a border with Switzerland
34 "___ said . . ."
35 Not single
36 Fixture in a doctor's office
37 Periodic law figs.
44 Change the borders of, say
45 Some pitch producers
46 Look a lot like
48 Dawdle
49 "___ l'amour"
50 2009 Wimbledon semifinalist Tommy
51 Best by a bit
52 Some branched pipes
53 Served the purpose
54 Urban trailer?
55 Went from soup to nuts, say
56 Syst. first implemented during W.W. I
57 Faze
58 Inits. of Ben Gunn's creator

by Tim Croce

117 HARD

ACROSS

1 "I'm a Survivor" sitcom
5 "West Side Story" girlfriend
10 Cabinet maker?: Abbr.
14 Icelandic saga subject
16 Long way to walk?
17 "Chantez-Chantez" singer, 1957
18 It's 180° from X
19 Cell division?
20 Places to put up
21 It's taken by some coll. seniors
22 Business brass
24 Some encumbrances
25 Class Notes subject, informally
27 "___ Gott, vom Himmel sieh darein" (Bach cantata)
30 Memorial Day performance
31 Almost in vain
36 Road locomotives
37 Runners often seen in windows
38 Big names
39 Poetic period
40 Idaho motto opener
41 Big guns in the Mideast
43 Norman with a legendary swing
45 Flying ___
46 Put away
50 Kosher's Islamic equivalent
53 Digital protection
54 Water flow regulator
56 Dip ___ in
57 Trafalgar Square figure
58 Lacking
59 Took home courses?
60 Salinger girl

DOWN

1 Hester Prynne's stigma
2 Journalist Burnett of 55-Down
3 Aid in judging distances
4 School rings?
5 Some patient responses
6 Beverage once sold "in all popular flavors"
7 Press
8 Coastal plunger
9 Some pitcherfuls
10 Southeast Asian soarer
11 Toasts
12 First name in 2000 headlines
13 Venting aids
15 Director Angelopoulos who won the 1988 Palme d'Or
23 The Five ___, 1950s million-selling doo-wop group
24 Slow passage
25 "___ baby!"
26 Singer learning a script
28 Bonehead
29 "Iceland" star, 1942
30 Function of some forks
32 1970s Thunderbird options
33 Rose family member
34 Waldorf-Astoria muralist
35 Tiger Express station brand
41 ___ Edibles (food shop on "The Facts of Life")
42 Spyder rival
44 South Korea's first president
46 Luzón, e.g.
47 Cardiological concern
48 River at Chartres
49 Conn of "Grease"
51 Its diameter is measured in picometers
52 Singer Lovich
55 Home of "Out Front"

by Martin Ashwood-Smith

ACROSS

1 Al Jazeera locale
10 Shot
15 2012 election issue
16 Set ___
17 Flip
18 Boss's directive
19 Mens ___
20 Soup flavorer
21 Source of some inside info?
22 Trouble in the night
24 Snarky reply after a lecture
26 W.W. II battle town
27 Bird named for its call
28 Foreign leader
29 Slip
31 Relishes
34 Leader given the posthumous title Rex Perpetuus Norvegiae
36 Trinity member
40 Jones's "Men in Black" role
44 Calculus, e.g.
45 Undercover wear?
48 Close up
49 Mates
50 Collegiate honor society of Bloomberg and Iacocca
53 Annie who voiced Bo Peep in "Toy Story"
54 Sticking points?

55 Cross reference?
57 Executed
58 Word with control or sight
59 Access provider
61 Some are bitter
62 Avalanche gear
63 Clipped
64 #1 on VH1's "40 Hottest Hotties of the '90s"

DOWN

1 Popular events for gamblers
2 The duck in "Peter and the Wolf"
3 It rates over 100,000 on the Scoville scale
4 Health advocacy abbr.
5 Grilling option
6 Berry variety
7 Nudist's lack
8 Shrinking body
9 Brief word
10 Noodles
11 '50s trial
12 Rock carrier
13 Dish containing masa
14 How one might speak
21 Where to pin a medal
23 First name in aviation

25 Major downer?
30 Taunt
32 Pause fillers
33 ___ Park, home of the San Diego Padres
35 Wedding wear
37 Spreadsheet command
38 Hockey shot involving two players
39 Story locale?
41 School grp.
42 Food whose name comes from the Tupi language of South America
43 "M*A*S*H" character from Toledo, Ohio
45 Military craft
46 "Pain Is Love" rapper
47 Beau
51 Big name in motels
52 Clean, in a way
53 What may represent "I" in American Sign Language
56 Game played across the world
59 Calculus abbr.
60 Setting in "Call of Duty: Black Ops," informally

by David Quarfoot

ACROSS
1 Field agents?
11 Amount to
15 Home of Owens Corning Corporation
16 First lady Harrison
17 Catchphrase of the '80s
18 Rock's Kings of ___
19 Big party
20 Big party
21 Coulrophobe's bugaboo
22 Extra turn in Monopoly
24 "Monster" actress, 2003
25 Explanatory lead-in
27 Composer/conductor Webern
28 What was yours at one time?
31 Puck, for one
33 Building with giant doors
35 Envy, anger or greed, maybe
36 Many a prom corsage
38 Napa Valley sight
39 Postal stamp on una carta
40 Patrick of "Barry Lyndon"
42 Dotted ones are half again as long
43 French cathedral city

48 Hard hits
49 Curly-haired toon
50 Possible result of an allergic reaction
51 Joe Hardy's girlfriend in the Hardy Boys books
52 What an ad blocker might block
54 Oater sound
55 Taking a load off
56 Big name in salad dressing
57 Current

DOWN
1 Shortchange
2 Duck and quail
3 "___ Walk" (Frost poem)
4 O'Connor of "Xena"
5 Setting for Yankees home games: Abbr.
6 Money-saving fast-food option
7 Nassau ___ liqueur
8 I = V/R
9 Accompanying
10 Like the K.G.B.: Abbr.
11 Excusing oneself from work, maybe
12 "Home on the Range" range
13 Treats to beat the heat
14 Kind of bed

21 Comparatively arch
23 Carnival booth with soda bottles
26 Jean, Jacques or Jean-Jacques
28 Like some paper punches
29 Do business?
30 They're usually found on the margins
32 Tomato
34 "Stand" band
36 "Walk On By" singer
37 Zesty casserole with a crust
41 Halloween personae
44 In the midst of
45 Overhauled
46 "The Vampire Diaries" girl
47 Rank smoke
49 Nobelist name of 1922 and 1975
52 D.E.A. target drug
53 Transportation for many a Little League team

by Mark Diehl

ACROSS

1 Mass merchandise?
7 A nerd has a low one
15 Side effect or ride effect?
16 Where to select Select All
17 Won't shut up
18 Far Eastern marinade
19 "Les Misérables" feature
20 Avian abductors
21 One goes along the 38th parallel, briefly
22 Protective zoo feature
23 49-Across maker
25 Wind sound
26 Unthreatening sorts
28 Don Diego de la Vega, familiarly
29 Dir. from 30-Across to Norfolk
30 See 29-Across
31 Some change in Russia
32 Ab follower
33 Aid in getting around
34 Brown drawer
37 Father figure?
38 Alternative to mushrooms
41 Puts some black lines on
42 Youngest member of a 1990s girl group
44 Sign of spotlessness
45 Leave
46 Like anatomical anvils
47 ___ Tech
48 Lightsaber user
49 23-Across product
51 Slowly came through
53 Chao of George W. Bush's cabinet
54 Characteristic of salts
55 Try to get off the straight and narrow
56 Thriller killer?
57 Pulling together, say

DOWN

1 They'll get you going with the flow
2 Like many a juke joint
3 Good place to lay down arms
4 Subject of I.R.S. Form 8949
5 It's noble
6 Natural Bridges State Beach locale
7 Fee
8 Some classic theaters
9 Around
10 Reply to "Really?"
11 Tan in a bookstore
12 Material for a slag furnace
13 Hard-to-remove stain
14 Chain serving Torpedoes and Bullets
24 It's deposited in drops
25 Betray dejection
27 Roars
28 Drops off, with "out"
31 About whom Obama said "He is a jackass. But he's talented"
32 New circulator of 2002
33 All-Century Team member
34 Breaks
35 Nice country house
36 They bear arms
37 Preprandial performance
38 Big Chilean export
39 Focus of some fairs
40 Ordered
42 Obfuscates
43 Mexican motel
45 Ushered
48 Simple gymnastics move
50 One way to direct a helm
52 Casino spot

by Barry C. Silk

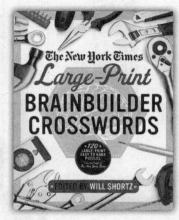
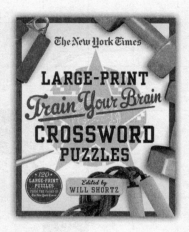

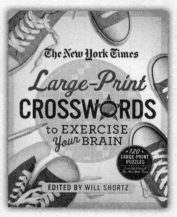

ANSWERS

1

```
B A H A █ E R A S E █ S G T S
E B O N █ L O R N A █ T O R O
G O H A L F S I E S █ A H E M
U V U L A █ A D E E █ R A K E
N O M O R E █ █ Z L O T Y █ █
█ █ G A L A X Y █ K I W I S
O R G Y █ I R E █ C A N I N E
N E O █ G O C R A Z Y █ R N A
T A B L E T █ O L E █ B E S T
O D E O N █ E X A C T A █ █
█ L A T E R █ H E D G E S
G O L F █ D R A G █ R H I N O
A S Y E █ G O C O M M A N D O
S L U R █ A R T O O █ I S E E
P O P S █ R S V P S █ R U D Y
```

2

```
B O G U S █ A S I A █ H T T P
U R I A H █ M A N S █ O H I O
M I R R O R O F T H E M I N D
R O D █ R E N E E █ S I N G █
A L L S T A R █ R A T E S █ █
P E E K █ C A S E W O R K E R
█ █ I S H █ A S S N █ I G O
H A I T I █ G U T █ I F N O T
E I N █ L E A N █ I A L █ █
P L A T E G L A S S █ A V E C
█ T O N G A █ A L A B A M A
█ B R U T █ X E B E C █ N I M
F A I R H A I R E D C H I L D
O N C E █ K E I R █ T O T I E
R E E D █ A S K S █ S P Y O N
```

3

```
C E L L O █ A M F M █ M E M O
A R I E L █ B O O P █ I R A N
B R E A D D O U G H █ S O N Y
S S N █ B I A S █ R A D I O
█ G A R R Y T R U D E A U
F L O A T E D █ O V I D █
A U D I █ A D E N █ I R A
W A I T I N G F O R G O D O T
N U N █ T A R T █ S E A M
█ E S A U █ C A E S A R S
M A R L O N B R A N D O █
E B O O K █ O R E G █ A P O
L I S P █ R E A R W I N D O W
O D I E █ U G L I █ E R A S E
N E E D █ M O D E █ R A M E N
```

4

```
Q V C   P S H A W   A N O D E
T E L   E P O C H   D I V E R
I R A   S A N T A M O N I C A
P O W D E R   S T A   E D I T
      U T E S     R A P
A L A B A M A S L A M M E R S
P E T A   E N T I T Y   L E O
L A T I N   D I M   L O V E R
U V A   D A R N I T   N E S T
S E R T A M A T T R E S S E S
      A K A     S O L E
F A R M   N U S   J I T N E Y
A M O A M A S A M A T   I D O
S M I L E   M A I N E   G A Y
T O L E T   C R A S S   H M O
```

5

```
E T H A N   B O M B S   T W O
T I A R A   A R I A L   E O N
C E N T S   S A L M O N R O E
E R G   M I M E   V O I D S
T R A F F I C A R T E R Y
C A R E L L     I N M A T E
    M A D A M S P E A K E R
I F S   R O I     I D S
R U L E S O F O R D E R
K R O G E R   O N E I L L
    P R E S I D E N T S D A Y
S W E E P   N E A T   U R N
L U S T A F T E R   O W N E D
O S U   S L E P T   M O N D O
E S P   T O R S O   S W O O N
```

6

```
L O L   O H S T O P   R O M E
A M I   R E P I N E   O J A Y
P E G   O L I V E R S T O N E
U G H S   E R O     O A S E S
P A T T O N O S W A L T
    S O D A     A M O E B A E
K H A K I   S E R F   O D D
R E B E C C A D E M O R N A Y
I R E   H G T S   P O E M S
S A R A L E E   D E N S
    M A R T Y F E L D M A N
A G A S P   A E C   O C T O
B E S T P I C T U R E   C P O
E R I E   N E E D E D   O A K
T E A L   T O S S E S   Y R S
```

7

P	I	P	P	I		A	S	O	F		A	D	Z	E
E	N	R	O	N		L	O	W	E		T	O	A	D
S	T	A	N	D	S	T	A	L	L		E	G	G	S
T	R	I	G		A	O	K		I	D	I	G		
L	A	S		K	I	S	S	A	N	D	T	E	L	L
E	Y	E	L	I	D			L	E	E		R	O	E
		E	N	H	A	L	O			F	E	L	T	
	H	A	N	D	I	N	T	H	E	T	I	L	L	
R	E	N	T			G	R	A	V	E	L			
A	M	A		I	R	R		I	A	M	S	A	M	
H	I	G	H	W	A	Y	T	O	L	L		U	Z	I
		R	O	O	M		I	C	E		E	T	A	S
A	R	A	B		J	E	T	H	R	O	T	U	L	L
L	I	M	B		E	L	L	E		P	A	R	E	E
P	O	S	Y		T	I	E	R		S	T	E	A	D

8

O	S	L	O		O	L	E	S		O	C	O	M	E
P	L	O	D		P	O	L	O		R	I	V	E	R
I	A	G	O		O	R	A	N		I	R	A	N	I
E	V	E	R	Y	S	I	N	G	L	E	C	L	U	E
				S	A	S		S	E	N				
A	R	T		P	U	F	F		A	T	L	A	S	T
L	A	I	T		M	O	R	E		A	I	S	L	E
I	N	T	H	I	S	P	U	Z	Z	L	E	H	A	S
A	O	L	E	R		S	I	R	E		D	E	N	T
S	N	E	E	R	S		T	A	P	S		S	T	Y
				I	S	M			P	E	A			
T	H	I	R	T	E	E	N	L	E	T	T	E	R	S
H	U	B	B	A		M	A	I	L		O	L	I	O
A	G	A	I	N		O	M	N	I		L	I	M	P
W	O	R	S	T		S	E	E	N		L	A	S	S

9

S	A	T	C	H		O	V	E	R	T		D	A	B
A	R	R	A	Y		D	A	R	E	R		E	D	U
B	E	A	R	(R)	E	D	L	A	(D)	Y		N	I	N
E	S	P	R	E	S	S	O		R	O	A	M	E	D
R	O	S	Y		S	(O)	R	T	I	N	G	(O)	U	(T)
			M	O	O	N		A	V	E	R	T		
W	A	K	E	N		E	X	E		O	H	O	K	
O	B	I		T	H	E	W	I	(R)	E		E	L	O
K	E	N	T		A	X	E		Y	A	R	D	S	
	G	I	M	L	I		I	B	E	T				
N	I	(C)	K	O	F	T	I	M	(E)		I	L	S	A
E	G	O	I	S	M		H	E	R	E	S	I	E	S
R	I	B		H	I	D	E	A	N	D	S	E	E	K
D	V	R		E	L	I	A	S		G	U	N	I	T
S	E	A		R	E	T	R	Y		Y	E	S	N	O

10

11

P	E	R	M	■	O	B	A	M	A	■	A	M	P	S
O	C	H	O	■	N	O	W	O	N	■	P	O	U	T
D	O	E	S	N	T	C	O	N	C	E	R	N	M	E
S	L	A	T	E	■	A	L	O	H	A	■	A	P	P
■	E	R	A	■	■	O	V	A	■	■	■	■	■	■
C	O	U	L	D	N	T	C	A	R	E	L	E	S	S
O	R	S	■	S	T	A	R	T	■	S	A	M	O	A
A	B	E	L	■	S	T	O	R	E	■	S	A	U	L
T	I	R	E	S	■	U	N	I	T	S	■	I	S	E
I	T	S	N	O	T	M	Y	P	R	O	B	L	E	M
■	■	S	A	W	■	■	■	E	A	R	■	■	■	■
S	P	A	■	M	A	F	I	A	■	P	I	K	E	S
N	O	S	K	I	N	O	F	F	M	Y	B	A	C	K
A	L	S	O	■	G	O	N	E	R	■	E	L	O	I
G	E	T	S	■	S	T	O	W	S	■	S	E	N	T

A	C	H	■	T	O	N	G	S	■	O	F	F	E	R
R	N	A	■	O	N	I	O	N	■	R	A	I	S	A
N	O	V	■	M	O	L	D	E	D	G	L	A	S	S
A	T	E	A	T	■	■	S	E	E	■	S	T	O	P
Z	E	A	L	O	T	S	■	Z	A	N	E	■	■	■
■	■	■	H	A	M	M	E	R	E	D	S	T	E	E	L
C	H	E	■	S	A	G	O	■	■	A	T	A	R	I
L	O	A	N	■	N	A	S	A	L	■	O	S	L	O
A	P	R	O	N	■	■	I	C	O	N	■	Y	E	N
P	E	T	R	I	F	I	E	D	W	O	O	D	■	■
■	■	■	T	A	L	C	■	C	E	N	S	O	R	S
S	U	C	H	■	O	E	D	■	■	U	S	E	U	P
C	R	U	S	H	E	D	R	O	C	K	■	S	N	L
A	G	R	E	E	■	U	N	D	U	E	■	I	I	I
R	E	L	A	X	■	P	O	E	T	S	■	T	N	T

12

O	V	E	R	■	M	A	U	L	■	P	O	W	E	R
V	E	R	A	■	E	R	T	E	■	A	R	E	S	O
A	G	O	G	■	A	L	O	T	■	M	E	N	S	A
L	A	S	T	S	T	O	P	■	S	P	O	T	O	N
■	■	A	T	L	■	I	K	E	A	■	■	■	■	■
■	M	A	G	O	O	■	A	I	R	S	P	A	C	E
Y	A	M	■	L	A	S	S	O	■	B	A	R	N	■
E	Y	E	L	I	F	T	■	S	E	T	S	H	O	T
A	B	B	A	■	O	S	K	A	R	■	E	N	S	■
H	E	A	D	L	O	C	K	■	R	E	A	D	Y	■
■	■	L	O	K	I	■	C	A	P	■	■	■	■	■
S	E	A	M	A	N	■	D	E	A	D	E	N	D	S
I	D	I	O	M	■	W	R	E	N	■	X	O	U	T
N	I	N	J	A	■	B	O	R	A	■	E	S	M	E
O	T	T	O	S	■	A	W	O	L	■	S	H	A	W

13

G	R	E	E	K	■	H	D	T	V	■	M	A	Z	E
M	I	A	M	I	■	Y	O	R	E	■	O	R	A	L
T	O	T	E	M	■	P	O	O	R	■	O	T	I	S
■	R	O	B	E	R	T	D	E	N	I	R	O		
■	S	P	I	N	E	■	■	U	N	R	E	E	L	
M	A	R	L	O	N	B	R	A	N	D	O	■		
E	L	O	■	S	E	R	U	M	■	S	C	H	W	A
A	V	O	N	■	T	U	N	I	S	■	K	A	H	N
L	O	F	A	T	■	N	I	N	A	S	■	N	I	T
■	V	I	T	O	C	O	R	L	E	O	N	E		
S	T	R	I	V	E	■	■	A	E	R	I	E	■	
T	H	E	G	O	D	F	A	T	H	E	R	■		
U	R	S	A	■	I	O	N	E	■	V	A	U	L	T
M	E	E	T	■	U	R	N	S	■	E	N	S	U	E
P	E	T	E	■	M	E	A	T	■	S	T	A	G	E

14

H	U	B	B	U	B	■	M	A	B	■	E	W	O	K
O	N	L	I	N	E	■	A	C	E	■	V	I	V	E
O	D	E	N	S	E	■	J	U	S	T	A	F	E	W
K	I	N	D	E	R	G	A	R	T	E	N	E	R	■
E	D	D	■	A	H	A	■	A	I	R	S	■		
■	F	L	A	P	S	■	R	E	V	A	M	P		
A	B	B	A	■	L	E	A	D	■	S	I	N	A	I
C	R	I	M	E	L	A	B	A	N	A	L	Y	S	T
T	I	E	I	N	■	T	O	R	A	■	L	A	S	H
S	E	L	L	T	O	■	T	W	I	C	E	■		
■	Y	A	N	K	■	I	L	L	■	I	S	O		
■	P	O	L	I	C	E	I	N	F	O	R	M	E	R
J	U	B	I	L	A	N	T	■	I	R	I	S	E	S
A	S	O	F	■	L	Y	E	■	L	O	V	E	M	E
W	H	E	E	■	L	A	M	■	E	X	E	T	E	R

15

E	L	K	■	F	E	D	■	■	M	O	V	I	N	G
V	A	N	I	L	L	A	■	R	E	C	I	T	A	L
E	C	O	N	O	M	Y	■	A	R	T	D	E	C	O
N	E	W	E	R	A	■	Y	W	C	A	■	M	R	S
■	I	V	A	N	H	O	E	■	V	A	S	E	S	
I	N	T	E	L	■	D	U	R	B	I	N	■	■	
L	I	A	R	■	I	T	S	■	R	A	I	L	E	D
E	L	L	■	H	A	V	A	N	A	N	■	O	L	E
S	E	L	D	O	M	■	I	O	N	■	C	O	S	A
■	D	O	S	I	D	O	■	D	A	K	A	R		
G	A	P	E	D	■	N	I	R	V	A	N	A	■	
A	P	E	■	W	H	A	T	■	I	T	A	L	I	A
L	A	T	V	I	A	N	■	A	T	E	D	I	R	T
A	R	R	A	N	G	E	■	C	A	R	A	V	A	N
S	T	I	N	K	S	■	E	L	S	■	E	N	O	

16

17

18

19

20

21

22

23

24

25

S	T	E	W		B	E	T	T	E		T	O	D	O
N	O	T	E		O	N	R	E	D		I	G	O	R
O	R	A	L		B	R	I	D	G	E	C	L	U	B
B	I	L	L	Y	B	O	B		E	N	T	E	R	S
		R	A	I	N		B	O	N	A				
C	A	V	E	R	N		B	L	U	E	C	R	A	B
A	P	I	A	N		B	A	I	T		O	N	O	
R	A	N	D	S		E	N	S		P	L	A	I	N
I	C	Y			P	A	D	S		R	I	N	S	E
B	E	L	L	Y	R	U	B		S	A	S	S	E	D
			I	V	E	S		D	E	N	T			
A	P	P	L	E	S		B	R	A	K	E	J	O	B
B	R	U	I	S	E	D	R	I	B		N	A	P	A
L	I	R	E		N	A	I	V	E		U	K	E	S
E	X	E	S		T	W	E	E	D		P	E	C	K

26

M	I	C	A	H		M	F	A	S		S	H	A	W
O	P	E	R	A		I	L	S	A		T	I	R	E
J	U	N	K	I	E	M	A	I	L		I	N	C	A
O	T	T		K	R	I	S			O	L	D	E	R
			Q	U	I	C	K	I	E	S	T	U	D	Y
R	E	B	U	S	E	S		N	U	T				
A	C	A	I				S	C	R	E	A	M	A	T
S	H	A	R	P	I	E	S	H	O	O	T	E	R	S
P	O	L	K	A	D	O	T			E	L	L	A	
			R	E	N		C	R	E	A	T	O	R	
B	E	A	N	I	E	S	P	R	O	U	T			
L	E	G	O	S		R	I	N	G		D	U	B	
O	R	E	O		B	O	O	K	I	E	C	A	S	E
O	I	N	K		L	U	B	E		N	O	T	E	S
P	E	T	S		T	R	E	Y		E	X	E	R	T

27

S	C	O	O	B		P	O	O	H		D	R	E	W
W	A	N	D	A		A	N	N	O		I	O	T	A
I	C	I	E	R		P	E	S	O		A	L	T	S
G	H	O	S	T	F	A	C	E	K	I	L	L	A	H
S	E	N	S	E	I		E	T	U	D	E			
			A	R	L	E	N	S	P	E	C	T	E	R
B	R	A		E	N	T			A	T	R	I	A	
R	U	G	R	A	T	S		K	I	S	S	E	R	S
O	T	H	E	R		C	I	V		Y	E	P		
S	H	A	D	O	W	B	O	X	I	N	G			
			S	N	E	A	D		E	A	R	T	H	A
D	I	S	T	I	L	L	E	D	S	P	I	R	I	T
O	K	L	A		O	L	I	O		P	L	A	N	S
P	E	A	T		S	E	N	T		E	L	I	D	E
E	A	V	E		T	R	E	E		D	E	L	I	A

28

```
A T B A Y ■ S H U S H ■ T B A
B R A C E ■ P U R E E ■ A R M
B E S T S H E L L E R ■ K I A
A X E L ■ A W L ■ ■ O M E N S
■ ■ ■ I F S ■ A L I A S E S
P I C K U P S H T I C K S ■ ■
O O H E D ■ C O O L ■ E T T U
D W I ■ D U R A N T E ■ O A S
S A V E ■ S E R E ■ M A C Y S
■ ■ A L L D A Y S H U C K E R
W I L L I A M ■ ■ E S C ■ ■ ■
E G R E T ■ ■ O H M ■ U C L A
I L O ■ M A R R Y I N S H A M
L O U ■ U N C A P ■ S E I Z E
L O S ■ S T A L E ■ A S P E N
```

29

```
D E B T ■ S I M P ■ Z A P S
V A L I D ■ U S E R ■ E U R O
D R O N E ■ C A S E ■ A R I A
■ ■ W A T C H T H E C L O C K
A D O ■ E A T ■ E M U ■ R E S
C O V E R T H E S P R E A D ■
T R E X ■ S A L ■ T E L ■ ■
S A R A N ■ T O T ■ S L U G S
■ ■ M O E ■ P A L ■ E N Y A
■ W A S H T H E L A U N D R Y
S A D ■ I C U ■ L I L ■ E O S
T U R N T H E C O R N E R ■ ■
A S I A ■ E V E N ■ A N W A R
R A F T ■ R O L E ■ S T A N D
R U T S ■ S S T S ■ ■ S Y N S
```

30

```
A P E ■ W H A M ■ C A J U N
H E X ■ E O N S ■ E O C E N E
A R P ■ S W I S S C H E E S E
■ G L E S S ■ I O N ■ P H D
V O O D O O D O L L ■ P E A L
A L I G N ■ I D O ■ V E R D E
T A T E ■ M E D ■ T E N S E D
■ ■ D A R T B O A R D ■ ■
E S T O P S ■ A L G ■ U Z I S
S P O U T ■ F L A ■ G L E N S
T A U T ■ G O L F C O U R S E
E T S ■ S I C ■ ■ R E M O P ■
F U L L O F H O L E S ■ I O S
A L E A S T ■ M O A T ■ N R A
N A D I A ■ Y O K O ■ G T O
```

31

32

33

34

35

36

37

```
GABS  OGRESS  FAD
REAM  APACHE  IRE
URGE  FALLENIDOL
FIELD    PAR  MGMT
FELLOWSHIP   PEAS
     YEOW  RABAT
ADO   RAW   ELISE
FILLINTHEBLANKS
LEDIN   OVO   GAP
    YOKED  INEZ
AMEN  FOLLOWSUIT
BALE  FLA   EATME
FULLNELSON   ZAHN
ARE  OCASEY  SHOD
BAR  STRODE  ANTS
```

38

```
BRR  DAVE   SWEAR
ROE  AGEE   HITTER
AND  DONCORLEONE
DARKAGE  MUD  DEL
    INS  THEBRIDGE
LAVA  NOEL  INSET
THERMO  REAVE
DAR  OVERTHE  RES
    NOONE  ARTIST
TWEEN  DRAB  ROPE
RIVERKWAI   SOB
ENE  INA  RATTRAP
ANNIVERSARY  ALI
TESTEE  ICON  VAT
ROARS  BENE   ONT
```

39

```
ZEST  GUT  KISSUPS
INCH  UNH  OCEANIA
OTOE  ESO  LETITBE
NOWHEREMAN   NOBS
    UNREAL  EAT
  GOLDENSLUMBERS
FOLK    WAIL  ILL
ANI  MICHELLE  CAY
NOV  ITOO   GENE
  WECANWORKITOUT
   OSO  KANSAS
COHN   REVOLUTION
HEYJUDE  ITE  ANDY
UNPOSED  NUT  LCDS
BOOBOOS  GPS  EASE
```

40

```
O H N O . . B R O . . T W O D
M O O R . S L O B . B O O R S
O T R O . C O L O . R O N D O
O L D S C H O O L . O T T O S
. . . C O M P S . H O T . . .
H O H O H O . K O M O D O . .
O R O . O S M O N D . O R R S
S L O P S . O S O . S T O O L
P O C O . M O T T S T . O N O
. P H O B O S . P R O L O G .
. . L O W . S T O O D . . . .
S C O R N . S N O O P D O G G
N O T O K . H O O K . L O O T
O C H O S . O W L S . O P T O
B O O M . . O S S . . T S O S
```

41

```
H A W K . O C T O . U M A S S
A G E E . H A R K . M U L C H
G R E A T A P E S . A S T O R
. . . S E R I O U S . H A R E
P O P . M E T . R U B Y R E D
C A R E . A L E N E . S D S .
P R O V A B L E . T H A . . .
. . W A R A N D P E A C E . .
. . N A T . T E A R D R O P
R P M . I S N O T . C O R E
C H A R L I E . P C S . S E Z
C O V E . N A M E O N E . . .
O N E A L . T H E D O N A L D
L E N T O . L O V E . I D I D
A S S A Y . Y S E R . D O V E
```

42

```
P A I L . S C T V . O R B E D
A R N O . A L O E . L E E R Y
R E A L K N O W L E D G E I S
M E L . L E S S . D E L T .
A L L H E R E . B A S E H I T
. . L A P . T O A S T . O R E
S T I N T S . T N N . S V E N
T O K N O W T H E E X T E N T
O N E A . I R E . R A I N E S
W I L . E V E R S . V P S .
S O I R E E S . O R I E N T S
. . H A L L . U N I E . I A L
O F O N E S I G N O R A N C E
W O O E R . A L E T . I T H E
N O D E S . N I T S . S H O P
```

43

F	R	A	U	D			S	E	A	R			C	O	T	S
A	N	D	S	O			O	R	C	A			A	F	E	W
B	A	S	S	R	E	L	I	E	F			N	C	A	A	
			R	E	L	I	C			S	T	O	A	T		
A	L	G		M	I	D	A	S	S	T	O	U	C	H		
R	O	O	M	I	E	S		I	T	E		R	T	E		
I	K	E	A			S	T	I	N	T	S					
D	I	S	C	U	S	S	T	H	R	O	W	E	R	S		
	B	E	R	T	H	S			A	N	A	T				
U	V	A		A	Y	E		A	W	E	S	O	M	E		
S	I	N	G	L	E	S	S	B	A	R		T	S	P		
O	R	A	L	S		A	U	T	O	S						
P	I	N	E		B	U	S	S	T	I	C	K	E	T		
E	L	A	N		A	S	H	E		C	A	L	V	E		
N	E	S	S		H	E	A	D		A	M	M	A	N		

44

I	S	T	O		Y	S	E	R		P	A	B	S	T
T	H	R	U		A	C	M	E		A	R	E	A	S
S	E	A	R	C	H	O	U	T		L	A	T	T	E
I	W	I	S	H		U	S	E	A	S	B	A	I	T
N	O	T		E	R	R		A	N	Y		C	D	S
	L	O	S	E	A	G	A	M	E		S	A	L	E
	F	R	A	Z	I	E	R		J	A	M	E	S	
		M	I	D	S	E	A	S	O	N				
D	E	P	O	T		U	N	A	S	K	E	D		
E	S	O	S		R	E	S	T	S	E	A	S	Y	
P	T	L		E	E	L		I	S	P		P	E	P
R	O	Y	A	L	S	E	A	L		H	O	O	T	S
E	N	S	U	E		C	E	L	T	I	C	S	E	A
S	I	C	E	M		T	R	E	K		H	O	S	T
S	A	I	L	S		S	O	S	O		S	S	T	S

45

T	A	B	S		T	H	A	I	S		I	N	R	E
E	C	R	U		W	A	N	N	A		N	E	A	T
A	T	O	P		O	S	K	A	R		A	E	R	O
M	A	K	E	R	S		L	I	O	N	S	D	E	N
		E	R	A		B	E	R	N	I	N	I		
S	A	N		T	E	E		G	R	A	N	T	S	
U	T	E		S	L	E	P	T		O	R	G	A	N
M	A	L	A		I	N	H	O	T		L	E	T	O
A	R	E	N	A		E	D	D	I	E		X	E	R
C	I	V	I	C	S		A	N	N		E	R	E	
	A	S	H	T	R	A	Y		O	R	R			
A	R	T	E	S	I	A	N		P	S	Y	C	H	E
C	O	O	T		F	L	I	N	T		D	I	E	T
M	A	R	T		F	L	O	R	A		E	S	M	E
E	R	S	E		S	Y	N	C	S		R	E	P	S

46

47

48

49

```
P A V L O V ■ T H E A ■ T V S
A G A S S I ■ I A G O ■ R A E
R E N T C O N T R O L ■ I L E
E S S ■ A L E U T ■ D C U P
■ G R E A S E M O N K E Y
A P T E S T ■ I S A K ■
A S W E ■ E R N S T ■ N I X
H A I R R E P L A C E M E N T
S T N ■ A M A S S ■ H E I R
■ C A R A ■ M T O S S A
C H I C A G O B E A R S ■
H A T H ■ R U S S O ■ A S I
O V I ■ C A T S P A J A M A S
M O E ■ H E H E ■ D A B O M B
P C S ■ E R O S ■ A N C I E N
```

50

```
A F F I X ■ A H E A D ■ D H S
S T O R K ■ B A S I E ■ E E L
P R O V E R B I A G E ■ T R E
H I T S ■ O A F ■ P E R O N
A L I ■ D I S A S T E R O I D
L E N T I L ■ M O R A I N E
T Y G E R ■ W O O F ■ S T E R
■ R E P A S T U R E ■
A C H S ■ R I S E ■ U R G E S
P H O E B E S ■ A B S E N T
P E R S I S T E R L Y ■ R D A
E D I T S ■ S O P ■ O M N I
A D Z ■ C O N Q U E S T I O N
S A O ■ A L E U T ■ A R E T E
E R N ■ Y A T E S ■ G O R E D
```

51

```
H T (M) L ■ B B C ■ E V A N
A R I (E) ■ A U R A E ■ C A G E
D A N C (E) C L A S S ■ O L A V
■ H O T (M) (E) S S ■ F I V E
L I N E N ■ (O) (N) O R D E R
O R O ■ S I R E ■ (A) T E A ■
B E T A ■ N O T A ■ H A T E S
O N E T W O T H R E (E) K I C K
S A L L Y ■ C E (C) E ■ S O L I
■ L E N D ■ L (O) N (G) ■ N A M
D O M I N O S ■ (M) A S T S
E S O S ■ W E I R D A (L) ■
E T T U ■ S E R P E N T (I) N E
D E E R ■ E D A M S ■ A T (N) O
S O L E ■ D Y S ■ R O W (E)
```

52

53

54

55

```
B L U R T S ■ ■ T H E L O T
R A N C H O ■ D E A R O N E
I M P A I R ■ C O R D O V A N
S A R ■ N E T H E R ■ S E R A
K N I C K ■ V A S E S ■ Y O N
E C C O ■ P S I S ■ U B O L T
T H E Q U E E N O F S O U L ■
S A D ■ N A T O ■ R A W ■
■ ■ E S C ■ F A I N ■ G L O
■ A R E T H A F R A N K L I N
D I E G O ■ N O O R ■ S A T E
E R S ■ P H N O M ■ B U R T S
N A P E ■ O O L A L A ■ E L I
I C E T R A Y S ■ A B I D E D
R E C T O R S ■ B Y N A M E
O S T E N D ■ S I F T E D
```

56

```
S P R I T E S ■ G O E S M A D
E R O T I C A ■ R A N W I T H
A I L E R O N ■ A T L A S E S
B E L M O N T S T E A K S ■
E S T S ■ I T I S I ■ U Z I
E T O ■ C O N A N ■ T S A R
■ P A R K I N G B R E A K S
P O I ■ R A T ■
C H O P P E D S T A K E S ■
O O H S ■ I T H E E ■ H O R
G E M ■ T O G A E ■ N A P A
■ S E R V I C E B R A K E S
C O L L E E N ■ D U E L E R S
O N A L E R T ■ G R A D U A L
B O W E D T O ■ E L L I P S E
```

57

```
C O M B S ■ E G G Y ■ R U S H
O N T A P ■ X T R A ■ I N C A
T E A S E ■ W O R K O F A R T
■ R I C C I ■ W E B E R
C R A C K O F D A W N ■ L E E
O U R ■ D E O R O ■ B E N D
C H A R M ■ G N O M E ■
A R T I C L E S O F F A I T H
■ E Q U A L ■ A N N I E
C O I L ■ A R E A S ■ A N D
A R C ■ B U N D L E O F J O Y
S I E G E ■ L E R O I ■
B O A R D O F E D ■ A D F E E
A L G A ■ A U R A ■ L O F T Y
H E E D ■ F R A Y ■ B R Y C E
```

58

59

60

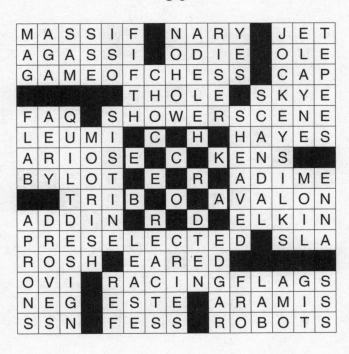

61

```
HENCE ▮ HOPS ▮ QUID
ALOHA ▮ ENTO ▮ UNDO
MILITARYASSAULT
ATIC ▮ TEX ▮▮ AIMEE
SEEKOUT ▮ ATTN ▮
▮ LABORPROTEST
PLAIT ▮ ISON ▮ BIB
LENT ▮ CASEY ▮ FATS
ENE ▮ RARE ▮ BUYUP
BOWLINGSCORE ▮
▮ OLEO ▮ ANALYZE
ADAGE ▮ ARC ▮ LOAM
NOJOYINMUDVILLE
OLAF ▮ DOES ▮ INKER
SERF ▮ ARNO ▮ MESSY
```

62

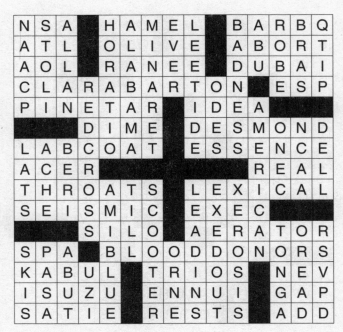

```
NSA ▮ HAMEL ▮ BARBQ
ATL ▮ OLIVE ▮ ABORT
AOL ▮ RANEE ▮ DUBAI
CLARABARTON ▮ ESP
PINETAR ▮ IDEA ▮
▮ DIME ▮ DESMOND
LABCOAT ▮ ESSENCE
ACER ▮▮ REAL
THROATS ▮ LEXICAL
SEISMIC ▮ EXEC ▮
▮ SILO ▮ AERATOR
SPA ▮ BLOODDONORS
KABUL ▮ TRIOS ▮ NEV
ISUZU ▮ ENNUI ▮ GAP
SATIE ▮ RESTS ▮ ADD
```

63

```
DAVE ▮ CHUNG ▮ OKRA
EMAG ▮ MALES ▮ HEED
FANG ▮ ONEUP ▮ INCA
ORDAINS ▮ TOBOOT ▮
GNARS ▮ OWETO ▮ GIA
SAL ▮ ULNAR ▮ OLAFS
▮ AZO ▮ DER ▮ AMYL
SQUAREDANCE ▮
BEAU ▮ MOD ▮ ZOE
SUMAC ▮ MITZI ▮ CSI
ARA ▮ AMANA ▮ REHAB
ONERUN ▮ IKEBANA
OPTS ▮ TITLE ▮ OREN
HOHO ▮ TAHOE ▮ LOSE
SPAS ▮ SNARL ▮ ANTZ
```

64

```
CAPO  PREOP  ESTD
ALEC  HASTO  LEER
SINK  ISITI  ILSE
SANAA EGON   GETS
ASANTE NITPICKS
VENDETTA BOOTIE
ASTR  AUTO  OUSTS
    OUTSIDERS
VIALS HOER  REDO
ANNLEE NAILEDUP
SETSSAIL SAFIRE
TROI  SKEW  COTAN
ERIN  INTOW RIBS
SONG  NOTRE MOLE
TREE  GWENS ENYA
```

65

```
CUBSWIN  ACADIAN
IPANEMA  COROLLA
ACMILAN  RCCOLAS
   DCCOMICS  BIT
PASEO  EDY  EENY
ECO MFAS  XFL
WCFIELDS  ATLAS
ERASMUS ACCOUNT
EASYA  JCPENNEY
  ETD  AERO  ENE
MUTT  ATV  FASTS
ANA  MCHAMMER
NCSTATE SEVENCS
OLEARYS EDITOUT
RESTYLE COLETTE
```

66

```
ITS  TRIPOD  SEA*
NEO  RENOIR  CLUB
CANDYAPPLE  RIGA
   ISLA  PIPESIN
FIRST*WAR  AWEEK
LAO  NROTC
OMAHAS ROOTCROP
ASMALL*AFTERALL
TOSSDOWN ONTIME
   REIGN  TAU
MATRI DEODORANT
UNHINGE MERE
MEIN  AWHOLENEW*
BERG GEARTO  GAL
OLD*  ABBESS  OXY
```

* = WORLD

67

A	R	M	O	R		I	B	M		S	C	A	D	S
W	O	R	D	S		D	U	E		C	O	U	R	T
G	A	Z	E	T	T	E	E	R		U	N	S	E	R
E	D	I	T		H	A	N	S	E	L		T	S	U
E	S	P	O	S	I	T	O		A	P	T	E	S	T
				O	R	E		A	S	T	O	R		
R	E	S	E	N	D		B	U	Y	S	T	I	M	E
E	V	E	R		C	R	O	S	S		I	T	I	S
B	E	A	R	C	L	A	W		T	H	E	Y	R	E
		H	O	R	A	S		M	R	I				
C	H	O	R	U	S		F	R	E	E	G	I	F	T
O	A	R		S	S	H	A	P	E		A	L	I	A
M	I	S	S	A		I	M	I	T	A	T	O	R	S
B	R	E	E	D		Y	E	N		B	O	N	E	S
O	S	S	I	E		A	R	K		E	R	A	S	E

68

J	U	N	O		P	C	B	S		S	M	A	S	H
A	T	A	N		A	R	I	A		H	I	R	E	E
G	E	N	E	O	L	O	G	Y		E	L	C	A	R
S	P	O	U	S	E	S		L	E	L	A	N	D	
		P	E	R	S	E	V	E	R	E	N	C	E	
I	S	M		M	E	R	C	I		N	E	E	D	
K	I	M	O	N	O		I	R	A	N	I			
E	X	E	C	S		M	C	S		B	U	D	G	E
			C	A	S	A	S		S	A	M	I	A	M
E	R	M	A		K	N	O	L	L		N	Y	U	
Q	U	E	S	T	I	O	N	A	I	R	E			
U	S	E	S	U	P		S	P	A	C	E	R	S	
A	S	T	I	R		M	I	S	P	E	L	L	E	D
L	I	M	O	N		S	M	E	E		A	L	B	A
S	A	E	N	S		U	S	S	R		T	E	A	K

69

R	A	B	B	I		T	A	S	K		J	O	G	S
O	N	I	O	N		O	S	L	O		A	P	O	P
S	E	T	T	H	E	P	A	Y	S		F	E	M	A
A	W	E		U	T	A	H		P	A	R	E	D	
		A	M	A	Z	I	N	G	G	R	A	Z	E	
M	A	M	M	A	L		I	R	A					
A	S	I	A	N		M	A	G	I		G	O	T	O
I	N	T	H	E	R	I	G	H	T	P	L	A	Y	S
N	O	E	L		E	T	A	T		R	E	T	R	O
			I	Z	E		S	E	N	S	E	S		
M	I	L	I	T	A	R	Y	B	A	Y	S			
A	M	A	S	S		U	R	D	U		H	U	B	
J	A	I	L		P	O	K	E	R	P	H	A	S	E
O	G	R	E		A	V	O	W		O	O	Z	E	D
R	E	D	S		C	A	N	S		N	E	E	D	S

70

```
Z I G S . K N O W . Q U I S P
I S E E . A R C H . U N T I L
S U I T E M A T E . I S E R E
T H E A S P . . L E T S E A T
. . . K A B U K I . E N I D .
S A W M I L L S . S R A . . .
E U R O P E A N S . E L O A N
R E P O M A N . E S T E L L E
E R A T O . C A T B A L L O U
. . O S S . S T A R D A T E .
I B A R . T A K E M E . . . .
B A I L E Y S . P A R A D E
M A F I A . C O U R T S H I P
A M A S S . A L V A . A P E X
C A R T E . P D A S . J U M P
```

71

```
M A H I M A H I . H I T C H Y
A M E N A M E N . E T A L I A
T O A S T I N G . L O M O N D
Z U L U . N E N E . P I T A .
O N E L . G A M I N . A S H Y
S T R A T A . A C E R . T I A
. . T O R E R O . A M E N D
A B S O R B S . L A C E R T A
G O E R S . P R O T E M . .
A R C . O P I E . A R O M A S
R A R A . R E T A N . R A V E
A B E D . I S O N . I R A N
G O T H A M . O N L O A N T O
A R E O L A . L I A R L I A R
R A S C A L . S E R A S E R A
```

72

```
U S E D C A R . T A L I B A N
G O N E A P E . W R I T E M E
A R T U R O S . O T O O L E S
N E W M A T H . I I N S I S T
D . I . V . O . R . C . E .
A S S H E . E G O S U R F S
N O T E L L . O N E B A S E
. R . E . S . P . E . C . T
. T E L S T A R . S L E E T S
. A S S I S T O N . E R N S T
. T . R . O . U . B . L . E
M E R I D E N . T R A V A I L
E X E C U T E . M I N I C A M
S P E A K E R . E S O B E S O
H O T N E S S . G E N E S I S
```

73

C	R	A	S	H		N	O	T	V			I	D	O
L	O	T	T	A		A	R	E	A	R		F	R	Y
E	L	T	O	N		V	I	N	D	I	E	S	E	L
A	L	E	C	G	U	I	N	N	E	S	S			
R	I	S	K		N	E	O		R	E	P	A	V	E
Y	E	T		D	I	S	C	O		S	A	B	E	R
			T	O	T		O	A	R		N	A	N	A
	O	B	I	W	A	N		K	E	N	O	B	I	
T	H	U	G		S	O	W		D	O	L			
L	I	G	H	T		L	A	D	D	S		N	B	C
C	O	S	T	E	D		L	E	O		L	A	R	A
		E	W	A	N	M	C	G	R	E	G	O	R	
L	O	A	N	E	R	C	A	R		I	C	A	N	T
A	N	D		S	T	A	R	E		N	A	N	C	E
X	E	D			H	A	T	E		D	R	O	O	L

74

A	T	O	M		H	O	N	O	R		S	L	U	M
L	O	G	E		A	R	E	N	A		C	O	R	E
B	I	R	M	I	N	G	H	A	M		A	S	I	S
A	L	E	P	P	O		I	N	A	F	L	A	S	H
			H	A	I	R			L	I	E	N		
H	A	S	I	D		I	O	N		O	R	G	A	N
A	L	A	S		S	A	M	O	A	N		E	M	O
B	A	N		A	T	L	A	N	T	A		L	O	O
I	M	A		A	N	T	H	E	M		D	E	C	K
T	O	N	E	R		O	A	T		B	E	S	O	S
			T	R	O	T			S	A	L	T		
D	O	O	R	N	A	I	L		S	U	R	G	E	S
E	D	N	A		C	R	O	S	S	R	O	A	D	S
J	O	I	N		K	O	R	E	A		I	B	E	T
A	R	O	D		S	N	E	A	D		T	E	N	S

75

O	P	I	E		O	B	I	E		B	E	I	N	G
B	A	N	D	S	T	A	N	D		E	M	C	E	E
I	T	S	G	O	T	A	G	O	O	D	B	E	A	T
S	H	O	A	L		B	O	M	B		A	R	T	
			R	A	B	A	T		E	R	R			
A	T	F		C	I	A		T	S	A	R	I	N	A
C	H	A	V	E	Z		T	E	E	N	A	G	E	R
T	E	R	A		A	N	D		S	L	O	E		
A	M	E	R	I	C	A	N		B	I	S	O	N	S
S	E	R	I	A	L	S		W	O	N		O	S	T
			A	N	O		S	H	O	A	T			
	S	O	N		W	A	N	E		S	I	M	M	S
Y	O	U	C	A	N	D	A	N	C	E	T	O	I	T
E	N	T	E	R		D	I	C	K	C	L	A	R	K
A	G	A	S	P		A	L	E	S		E	N	O	S

76

S	H	I	A	T	S	U	■	■	S	T	R	I	F	E
M	ELO	N	B	A	L	L	■	C	H	E	E	S	ELO	G
A	I	L	E	R	O	N	■	H	A	N	G	I	N	G
L	S	A	T	■	S	A	B	E	R	S	■	S	Y	S
L	E	W	■	R	H	E	A	■	P	E	W	■		
■	■	I	C	Y	■	N	E	W	S	H	O	L	E	
I	V	A	N	A	■	M	D	V	I	■	O	N	I	N
M	ELO	T	T	■	C	U	B	I	T	■	O	C	ELO	T
A	U	T	O	■	O	T	O	E	■	S	P	E	W	S
T	R	A	I	L	M	I	X	■	P	A	S	■		
■	T	A	B	■	E	P	I	C	■	T	A	P		
E	F	T	■	B	I	A	S	E	S	■	R	O	N	I
R	E	A	G	A	N	S	■	A	T	L	A	R	G	E
R	ELO	C	A	T	E	S	■	C	O	U	N	S	ELO	R
S	K	O	R	T	S	■	■	E	N	V	I	O	U	S

77

F	L	I	P	■	K	E	I	R	A	■	V	E	N	I
I	O	N	O	■	E	X	C	E	L	■	A	V	O	N
E	N	C	H	A	N	T	E	D	I	S	L	A	N	D
F	I	L	L	M	O	R	E	■	O	U	N	C	E	
■	■	I	B	A	■	M	A	L	E	S	E	X		
L	Y	M	E	D	I	S	E	A	S	E	■			
S	O	R	T	S	■	N	U	I	■	A	M	P	S	
T	H	E	A	T	R	E	D	I	S	T	R	I	C	T
S	O	D	S	■	A	N	I	■	O	O	M	P	A	
■	P	I	C	T	U	R	E	D	I	S	C			
R	O	S	W	E	L	L	■	S	E	T	■			
A	B	O	R	T	■	D	E	L	A	W	A	R	E	
J	E	D	I	S	T	A	R	F	I	G	H	T	E	R
A	L	A	S	■	B	R	A	U	N	■	O	R	E	L
H	I	S	T	■	S	A	B	L	E	■	S	I	D	E

78

■	A	D	O	L	P	H	■	H	E	A	P	O	N
I	B	E	F	O	R	E	■	E	E	X	C	E	P	T
G	O	L	F	T	O	U	R	N	A	M	E	N	T	S
N	Y	E	T	■	A	R	I	S	T	A	■	S	O	B
■	H	O	M	E	S	■	E	T	A	■				
O	L	S	E	N	S	■	I	N	D	E	N	T	
N	I	E	C	E	■	A	N	A	L	■	C	H	I	P
C	E	I	L	I	N	G	■	H	Y	G	I	E	N	E
E	N	Z	O	■	H	U	T	S	■	W	E	I	R	D
■	E	C	O	L	A	W	■	G	E	N	R	E	S	
■	K	N	T	■	I	D	O	N	T					
O	W	E	■	L	E	T	S	U	P	■	R	A	M	S
R	A	D	I	O	A	S	T	R	O	N	O	M	E	R
B	I	G	N	A	M	E	■	R	O	O	M	E	R	S
S	T	E	E	N	S	■	A	F	T	E	R	C	■	

79

```
N A P A . J A W . A S I D E S
O M E R . E X O . T H R O W N
M A N P O W E R . H O T T E A
A Z T E C S . S P E W . M L I
D E A L T . S T O N E W A L L
. S O Y A . M A R A T .
A I M . P I N T . I R A Q
P L A Y I N G W I T H F I R E
B A J A . O S S A . X E D
. O R T H O . L A N G .
B I R D H O U S E K E L S O
U N E . R O I L . S I L E N T
L O T S O F . A N T E A T E R
B U T A N E . V I A . T H R O
S T E W E D . E B B . O E D S
```

80

```
S A D . M E D I C . K N O B S
N O E . A X I A L . A S C O T
A N A S T A S I A . T A T A R
R E D R U M . M I R Y . A T E
. W A R P S . R E D A N E S
F A O . E L O I . B I P E D S
I G O T . E N N E A D S .
R E D U P . I S P . S E R I F
. T R A C H E A . S I R E
F O S T E R . R E D S . G A D
I L L O G I C . S A I T H
L E I . N A H S . P R O T O N
M O C H A . E A R T H T O N E
C L E A N . E V I T A . N C R
R E D I T . R E D O N . R E D
```

81

```
E M M A . H O B O . A H A N D
S A I L . A L E C . V O I C E
S I N G I N G T E L E G R A M
A N I O N . A W A Y . S P A S
Y E A R N S . E N E S C O
. T E E H E E . S T O R M S
S H U . R E I N S . O R T O N
M A R I E A N T O I N E T T E
E L E N A . S H I R E . E T E
E S C A R P . E L A T E R
. A S S A I L . N O R M A L
M C M L . P R I M . O R I B I
A L E U T I A N I S L A N D S
N U R M I . T E S H . T A U T
N E A P S . E S T E . A L L S
```

82

M	E	S	A	S	■	P	A	R	M	■	■	C	I	G
O	U	T	D	O	■	S	T	E	E	P	F	I	N	E
O	W	E	M	E	■	Y	O	M	T	V	R	A	P	S
D	E	V	O	U	R	■	L	U	S	C	I	O	U	S
■	E	N	R	O	L	L	S	■	P	E	S	T	O	■
T	U	N	I	S	I	A	■	R	I	D	■	■	■	■
A	H	A	S	■	■	S	H	E	E	P	■	N	I	H
P	U	S	H	T	H	E	E	N	V	E	L	O	P	E
A	H	H	■	H	A	R	P	O	■	■	A	P	S	E
■	■	■	L	U	G	■	■	R	A	G	W	E	E	D
B	A	C	O	N	■	A	A	M	I	L	N	E	■	■
A	M	Y	A	D	A	M	S	■	R	A	C	K	U	P
L	I	S	T	E	R	I	N	E	■	Z	A	I	R	E
S	E	T	H	R	O	G	E	N	■	E	R	N	S	T
A	S	S	■	■	D	A	R	T	■	D	E	G	A	S

83

S	H	A	M	E	D	■	■	C	H	I	M	E	R	A
W	E	C	A	R	E	■	S	H	A	D	O	W	E	D
A	L	E	G	A	R	■	C	A	R	O	T	E	N	E
P	O	L	I	T	I	C	A	L	D	N	A	■	■	■
S	T	A	C	■	G	I	N	K	G	O	■	A	M	S
■	■	■	B	L	U	N	T	S	■	T	S	L	O	T
S	T	B	E	D	E	■	Y	U	L	■	P	L	O	Y
T	O	T	A	L	U	P	■	P	O	T	H	O	L	E
O	W	E	N	■	R	E	F	■	A	K	I	T	A	S
L	E	A	S	T	■	P	L	A	N	O	N	■	■	■
E	L	M	■	R	E	S	O	L	E	■	X	T	R	A
■	■	■	J	A	C	Q	U	A	R	D	L	O	O	M
P	A	R	A	M	O	U	R	■	C	O	I	N	O	P
F	A	I	R	P	L	A	Y	■	A	L	K	A	N	E
C	R	O	S	S	E	D	■	R	E	E	L	E	D	■

84

■	■	R	I	P	■	■	■	S	A	W	■
■	G	O	P	R	O	■	S	E	L	I	G
G	A	L	L	I	U	M	■	C	H	A	I	N	E	D
A	L	L	A	N	T	E	■	L	A	S	C	A	L	A
S	A	I	N	T	V	A	L	E	N	T	I	N	E	S
■	S	E	T	S	O	N	E	A	T	E	A	S	E
■	■	O	U	T	S	T	R	I	P	S	■
V	A	C	■	P	E	N	S	E	E	S	■	M	M	L
E	N	A	S	■	D	O	D	D	S	■	P	E	A	L
S	T	R	A	P	■	T	I	L	■	E	E	N	I	E
T	E	N	D	E	R	H	E	A	R	T	E	D	L	Y
A	D	E	L	P	H	I	■	N	E	A	R	E	S	T
L	U	R	E	S	I	N	■	E	S	P	A	R	T	O
S	P	A	R	I	N	G	■	S	T	E	T	S	O	N

85

```
B A B E M A G N E T ■ R E S P
E L I W A L L A C H ■ E X P O
A F T E R T A S T E ■ C H A W
M A S ■ B A N A ■ S E A I C E
■ ■ S L I D ■ S T A P L E R ■
S I F T E R ■ C L A S S A C T
C H A D S ■ B L U N T ■ R A O
H A L S ■ F R I E D ■ D A D O
O D S ■ N O U N S ■ B E T E L
O N E T O O N E ■ V A L E T S
L O S E S T O ■ H I N T ■ ■ ■
M I T T E N ■ F E E D ■ S P F
A D A R ■ ■ O W E N W I S T E R
T E R A ■ T H E R E T H E R E
E A T S ■ E A S Y D O E S I T
```

86

```
R O A S T E R S ■ T U S H E S
O N T H E L A M ■ I N L O V E
C A L A M I N E ■ M A R L E E
O P A ■ P A S T I E S ■ D A S
C A S C O ■ H A I R ■ O O R T
O R T H ■ L O N I ■ W A N D A
■ ■ ■ A G O R A ■ N A T T E R
S W A P O U T ■ S E R M O N S
T I G E R S ■ T H E M E ■ ■ ■
A S N A P ■ A R O D ■ A G O G
T H O U ■ I M U S ■ I L O N A
E B S ■ R H Y T H M S ■ R B I
P O T S I E ■ H O O L I G A N
E N I G M A ■ I N R E P O S E
N E C T A R ■ S E A S O N E D
```

87

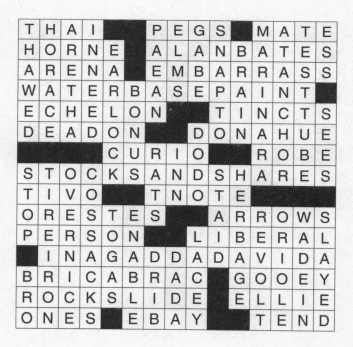

```
T H A I ■ P E G S ■ M A T E
H O R N E ■ A L A N B A T E S
A R E N A ■ E M B A R R A S S
W A T E R B A S E P A I N T ■
E C H E L O N ■ T I N C T S
D E A D O N ■ D O N A H U E
■ ■ ■ C U R I O ■ R O B E
S T O C K S A N D S H A R E S
T I V O ■ T N O T E ■ ■ ■
O R E S T E S ■ A R R O W S
P E R S O N ■ L I B E R A L
■ I N A G A D D A D A V I D A
B R I C A B R A C ■ G O O E Y
R O C K S L I D E ■ E L L I E
O N E S ■ E B A Y ■ T E N D
```

88

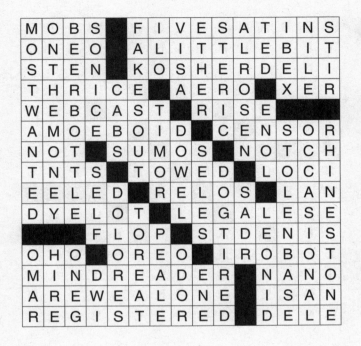

89

90

91

```
H O T S P E L L   S T I L T S
A C H I E V E S   H O H O H O
M E A T D I E T   O R A T E S
F A T C A T S   B E I T S O
I N S O L E   R A S A E
S L A M S   C A N T M I S S
T I N S   S A W T O O T H E D
E N O   G A N D E R S   O D O
D E N T A L C A R E   C R I P
  R O O T L E T S   T H E M E
    P H Y L A   V O I L E S
  L A S E R S   S A R G E N T
H E G I R A   R E L E G A T E
I C E D I N   I L L N E V E R
T H E E N D   M A I T R E D S
```

92

```
E B B A N D F L O W   W I T S
L E A V E A L O N E   W R A P
I N T E R L I N E D   I A G O
S T A N D I N G A G A I N S T
H O A G Y   T A L E S   G A P
A N N E   F I G S   T R A L A
      O R E O   G R A T E S
S H O C K E R   P R O W E S S
W A R N E D   D Y E S
I R E N E   A I R Y   G I B E
L P S   F A L D O   F I N E S
L E T T E R B O X F O R M A T
I D E A   G I V E O R T A K E
N O I R   O N E N I G H T E R
G N A T   S O R E L O S E R S
```

93

```
T H E B B C   S P A C E J A M
H I L A R Y   C O C A C O L A
A M I N U S   O K A Y O K A Y
W O M A N   P R I C E L E S S
  M A N E   L E N I N
    N A I V E   G A N D A L F
S I N S   A B A   E A S E L
T O I L   T E C H Y   V I N E
A N N U M   T O E   E A S E
G A G G I F T   R A M E N
      L O O P S   E G G S
M A S T E R K E Y   A G A P E
A L P H A B E T   A N E M I A
C I A A G E N T   D I R E C T
H E N N E S S Y   M E S S E S
```

94

```
P O T S M O K E ■ D I S C U S
O N E L I T E R ■ A L E A S T
P A S Y S T E M ■ T E X T M E
A S T ■ T E P I D ■ A T T A R
P P P S ■ R E N E W ■ O L I O
I R A T E ■ R E B E L Y E L L
L E G A T O ■ S I L A S ■ ■ ■
L E E ■ H A M ■ T L C ■ U P A
■ ■ ■ S O S A D ■ S E A S O N
P R A I S E G O D ■ S N E R D
P E L L ■ S O W E D ■ E R N S
P A L E S ■ O N S E T ■ N S C
P L I N K O ■ L A T E D A T E
P I E T I N ■ O D E T O M A N
P A S H T O ■ W E R E H E R E
```

95

```
M A M M A S ■ T O P P R I Z E
A V I A T E ■ U N L O O S E N
M E D G A R ■ X M A S C A R D
B R A I N F R E E Z E ■ B O S
O T I C ■ ■ E D D A ■ P E E L
S S R S ■ K A O S ■ G O L D A
■ ■ Q U A D S ■ S U N L I T
M A T U R E S ■ B E N Z E N E
I S H A L L ■ B R A S I ■ ■ ■
Y O U R S ■ M R I S ■ S C A T
A N N E ■ S O O N ■ C L U E
Z E D ■ J E R S E Y S H O R E
A M E N A M E N ■ O P E N O N
K A R E N I N A ■ N A M E R S
I N S E A S O N ■ D R E D A Y
```

96

```
H O T P A S T R A M I ■ A N E
I S A A C A S I M O V ■ B O X
P E T S E M A T A R Y ■ P I C
S S E ■ T O R E ■ A R I O S I
■ ■ B A S S ■ S Y O S S E T
S O N A T A ■ D O E S T I M E
A D E L E ■ S A R E E ■ T A M
L E W D ■ B E Z E L ■ M I K E
A R F ■ R A C E R ■ R A V E N
D N A T E S T S ■ D E S E R T
G E N E S E S ■ W E T S ■ ■ ■
R I G S U P ■ S H A Y ■ F A R
E S L ■ M A S T E R P I E C E
E S E ■ E T H E L M E R M A N
N E D S H O W M E S T A T E
```

97

```
A D O P T I O N █ A R I S E S
N O N E E D T O T H A N K M E
I M E A N I T T H I S T I M E
T E A S █ █ █ M A N T O M A N
A S S E Z █ S Y N T A X █
█ █ █ █ E S E █ █ I S T H
T R I P L E W O R D S C O R E
R E S I D E N T I A L A R E A
I M I T A T I O N B U T T E R
B E A T S O N E S B R E A S T
E T H S █ █ █ E A P █ █
█ █ B A L L A D █ S T E A M
P E C U L I A R █ █ A N T E
O P E R A T I O N C O N D O R
L O N G T E R M P A R K I N G
E S T H E R █ A R R E S T E E
```

98

```
M I C A █ A L I E N R A C E S
A D A M █ M E A D O W L A R K
D O L P H I N S A F E T U N A
E M I L E █ T I M E █ S T E T
R E F E R S █ M S E C █ I S E
O N O R █ N G O █ S O H O T █
O E R █ R E A V E █ Z I N █
M O N K E E S █ T H E C A R S
█ █ I L L █ X E N O N █ R E W
█ T A M I L █ T A W █ T Y P E
R I G █ C U T E █ L I O T T A
A V I S █ M A R T █ C L A I R
P O R C U P I N E Q U I L L S
I L L U M I N A T E █ F E E T
D I S M A N T L E D █ E S S O
```

99

```
M A I L B A G █ █ T O W N E
A L L O R N O N E █ A P H I S
G O L D E N B O Y █ P I O N S
I N B E D █ A T R A █ E L E A
C E E S █ O N M E D S █ E L Y
█ █ █ B A Y █ D O G S I T
B R I M █ O N C E █ S U A V E
L A C A G E A U X F O L L E S
O R A T E █ S P C A █ P E S T
W E N T O N █ O L D █ █
A G T █ S N A F U S █ F L A W
F A W N █ E S T S █ P L A N A
U S A I D █ S E I Z E U P O N
S E I K O █ N A V A L B A S E
E S T E S █ █ E G E S T E D
```

100

```
D I O R A M A ■ A C T A B L E
I M N O T I N T E R E S T E D
P R I C E O N O N E S H E A D
S E T S ■ ■ W E S T E N D ■
■ ■ N O T E A S Y ■
D I S C O L O R S ■ ■ A C H E
I N T E N D T O ■ L A S H E S
C H A N C E O F S U C C E S S
T O T T E R ■ L A C R O S S E
A C E S ■ C O W R I T T E N
■ ■ S C A N N E D ■ ■
■ B I G H A N D ■ I E S T
H A V E A G O O D M I N D T O
A B E R D E E N T E R R I E R
N E S T E R S ■ S T K I T T S
```

101

```
G I V E M E O N E R E A S O N
I N O N E S S A L A D D A Y S
S O W H A T E L S E I S N E W
T I T A N S ■ S T I R ■
■ L O N ■ E E N ■ E T A I L
■ C R A N N Y ■ D E F O E
■ F R E E S T A T E ■ S A W N
W T O ■ C O W B I R D ■ E A T
E L O I ■ F I L M R E E L S
L E F T S ■ N E E S O N ■
L E T H E ■ E R S ■ I S T
■ R U M P ■ R A G T O P
Y O U R P L A C E O R M I N E
I N S T R U M E N T P A N E L
P A S S E S O N D E S S E R T
```

102

```
U P D R A F T S ■ A P I C A L
S E E A B O V E ■ P O C O N O
A T M C A R D S ■ P O E T I C
B R U I S E R S ■ T H R E S H
L O R N E ■ A I D ■ S I R E N
E L S E ■ A M O R E ■ N I T E
■ J E A N J A C K E T S
S P A D E S ■ T O S S E S
T H E O D O R E R E X ■
E A R N P A L I N ■ A B C S
P L O T S ■ G M T ■ E G R E T
F A S C E S B A T P H O N E
O N T A P E A L I C A N T E
U G A R T E R I P O S T E D
R E R E A D ■ K N O T T E R S
```

103

A	L	I	B	A	B	A	█	█	█	A	S	K	T	O
S	O	D	A	J	E	R	K	S	█	B	L	E	E	D
C	A	L	L	I	N	G	I	N	█	C	O	P	A	Y
O	N	E	E	G	G	█	N	E	O	█	A	T	M	S
T	S	R	█	█	A	L	D	E	R	█	N	A	P	S
█	█	V	A	L	O	R	█	G	O	E	T	H	E	█
█	D	I	E	S	█	R	E	H	A	B	█	B	O	Y
L	I	K	E	H	E	R	D	I	N	G	C	A	T	S
E	A	N	█	E	G	E	S	T	█	Y	O	Y	O	█
G	L	O	S	S	Y	█	P	O	I	N	T	█	█	█
A	T	W	O	█	█	P	A	I	N	T	█	█	S	H	E
L	O	I	N	█	T	O	R	█	L	E	A	P	O	N
A	N	T	I	C	█	█	K	I	L	L	S	T	I	M	E
G	E	I	C	O	█	S	T	U	D	P	O	K	E	R
E	S	S	E	X	█	█	█	N	O	N	Z	E	R	O

104

S	Q	U	A	B	B	L	E	█	L	A	R	E	D	O
A	U	N	T	I	E	E	M	█	E	L	O	P	E	D
N	A	K	E	D	A	S	A	J	A	Y	B	I	R	D
D	Y	N	A	S	T	█	N	U	N	N	█	S	I	S
A	L	O	T	█	B	E	A	S	T	█	P	O	S	H
L	E	T	█	W	A	N	T	T	O	█	I	D	I	O
█	█	N	A	C	R	E	S	█	A	L	E	V	E	█
M	A	Z	U	R	K	A	█	A	T	L	A	S	E	S
I	D	A	R	E	█	P	R	Y	O	F	F	█	█	█
S	E	N	S	█	S	T	A	I	R	S	█	D	U	N
S	N	E	E	█	Q	U	I	N	T	█	S	U	P	E
T	A	G	█	B	U	R	N	█	U	P	E	N	D	S
A	U	R	O	R	A	E	B	O	R	E	A	L	I	S
R	E	E	K	E	D	█	O	V	E	R	T	A	K	E
T	R	Y	S	T	S	█	W	I	D	E	O	P	E	N

105

C	O	I	N	█	S	H	I	R	T	█	C	A	R	P
A	N	N	A	█	C	A	M	E	O	█	O	L	E	O
S	T	A	M	P	O	F	A	P	P	R	O	V	A	L
T	H	R	E	E	T	I	M	E	S	A	L	A	D	Y
█	E	R	S	A	T	Z	█	O	A	T	E	R	S	█
S	M	E	A	R	Y	█	S	P	I	E	D	█	█	█
L	E	A	K	Y	█	J	E	L	L	S	█	P	I	P
I	N	R	E	█	T	A	X	E	S	█	C	A	N	E
M	D	S	█	P	A	C	E	D	█	M	A	R	T	A
█	█	S	I	L	K	S	█	M	E	R	K	E	L	█
█	C	H	A	L	K	S	█	K	U	R	T	I	S	█
D	R	A	W	A	T	T	E	N	T	I	O	N	T	O
E	A	S	Y	F	O	R	Y	O	U	T	O	S	A	Y
A	N	T	E	█	M	A	R	L	A	█	N	O	T	E
D	E	E	R	█	E	W	E	L	L	█	Y	N	E	Z

106

```
C H O C O L A T E M O U S S E
E A T O N E S H E A R T O U T
N U R S E C L I N I C I A N S
T S O ■ ■ H A S ■ M A C ■ ■ ■ ■
O A S I S ■ N I T ■ S A R A S
■ ■ ■ R E M ■ S I D ■ ■ E P A
I N T E R N A L A U D I T O R
M A I N T E N A N C E F R E E
M A K E A M E N T A L N O T E
I C K ■ ■ E N D ■ T O O ■ ■ ■
E P I C S ■ T E E ■ S T A P H
■ ■ U A E ■ A L E ■ ■ P E U
T A K E N O P R I S O N E R S
A H A R D N U T T O C R A C K
R A I S E S T H E S T A K E S
```

107

```
S M E W ■ J A W S O F L I F E
I A T E ■ E A R L Y R I S E R
X K E S ■ W H I R L Y B I R D
E E R ■ M E E T ■ ■ P E N N A
R U N W I L D ■ M E A L ■ ■
S P I E L S ■ B A R N ■ S E P
G E T I T ■ T E X A S S T A R
A X I L ■ A E G I S ■ P A S O
M A E L S T R O M ■ C A N T S
E M S ■ T O R T ■ D R Y M O P
■ ■ S U Z Y ■ M E A S U R E
B R E A D ■ M O A B ■ S A C
R U B B E R S O U L ■ T I N T
O D E R N E I S S E ■ R A G U
W I N E T A S T E R ■ A L E S
```

108

```
I G O O F E D ■ B O B S T A Y
S A N T I N I ■ O P U S O N E
A M B A N D S ■ R E S T O N S
I B O ■ S E A S A L T ■ C R I
D R A C ■ D R U B S ■ P O U T
S E R U M ■ M N O ■ A I O L I
O L D P A L ■ G R I Z Z L E S
■ C R A N ■ A N T Z ■
A Q U A T E E N ■ B E A V E R
B U C K Y ■ H E T ■ C Z E C H
S I D E ■ M I X I T ■ Z A L E
O R A ■ A U S T E R E ■ L I B
L I V E S T O ■ R I V E R P O
U N I F I E D ■ O B E L I S K
T O S T A D A ■ D E L I B E S
```

109

```
P A S S I O N P I T ■ O A F S
O P E N S O U R C E ■ H U L U
R E C O R D D E A L ■ O D I C
C R O W ■ L E T M E T H I N K
■ ■ A V E ■ E X E ■ D T S
I N U N I S O N ■ E L W E S ■
B A N G S ■ H A R D ■ H A T E
E M C E E ■ I D O ■ P Y L O N
T E L L ■ T O I L ■ F I E N D
■ C E S T A ■ R E S C O R E S
J A R ■ I N C ■ A S U ■
E L E N A K A G A N ■ G I N O
A L M A ■ T I E F I G H T E R
N E U T ■ O N E A T A T I M E
E R S E ■ P E R R Y M A S O N
```

110

```
S P I L L A G E ■ A T B E S T
H O N E Y B U N ■ S O O N Y I
A L T E R A N T ■ T U B I N G
M A S T I F F S ■ O R B A C H
■ I S T O ■ N A C H T
L I N D T ■ R A C I E R ■
O T O E ■ T H I R T Y R O C K
L A T ■ S A I D Y E S ■ X I I
A L I N E D R E S S ■ F E T A
■ B A S E S T ■ N I N E S
S T E A D ■ A L A R ■
H A N G E R ■ P L A T E A U S
O C T A V O ■ I S T H A T S O
P E R M I T ■ G E T A N T S Y
S T E E L E ■ S T E N T O R S
```

111

```
A T M S ■ M M M B O P ■ S P Y
T R I P ■ O M E R T A ■ T I O
M I S E ■ W I R I E R ■ R E N
O F F E N S I V E R E M A R K
S L I C E ■ F I N A N C E
T E T H E R E D ■ T I G E R
■ D O N U T S ■ Z E D S
■ C O S M O K R A M E R ■
M C A N ■ P L E A S E ■
R O L E X ■ S P E C T A T E
S T O P G A P ■ C O L I N
P E R M A N E N T M A R K E R
A R I ■ M E T E O R ■ S A R A
U I E ■ E N C O R E ■ O L E G
L E S ■ S T O N E D ■ S I D E
```

112

	C	A	L	I	C	O	C	A	T			A	R	A	L
B	A	N	A	N	A	R	A	M	A			M	I	M	I
A	S	T	R	O	N	O	M	I	C			O	P	A	L
S	H	O	R	N			I	G	O	C	R	A	Z	Y	
T	I	N	Y		G	A	L	O	S	H		P	O	P	
A	N	Y		J	A	I	L	S		I	V	A	N	A	
			F	O	R	M	A		M	A	D	R	I	D	
M	A	D	L	I	B	S		P	I	N	A	T	A	S	
A	Q	U	I	N	O		G	U	S	T	Y				
L	U	M	P	S		C	O	N	T	I		M	A	W	
C	A	B		I	B	O	O	K	S		G	A	L	A	
O	R	D	I	N	A	L	S		F	O	R	D	S		
L	I	O	N		S	L	I	P	P	I	N	G	O	N	
M	U	R	K		H	A	N	G	I	N	G	O	U	T	
X	M	A	S		O	R	G	A	N	I	S	T	S		

113

R	E	G	A	L	I	A			C	S	H	A	R	P
E	V	A	D	E	R	S		U	L	T	I	M	A	S
S	E	I	Z	E	O	N		N	E	A	T	E	N	S
I	N	T	E	R	N	E	T	D	A	T	I	N	G	
Z	E	E	S		B	E	H	A	N		T	A	T	A
E	R	R		S	A	D	E	Y	E	D		M	R	S
			S	T	R	E	P		D	U	D	E	U	P
I	S	S	U	E		D	E	M		V	I	N	E	S
C	A	T	N	I	P		Q	A	T	A	R			
E	V	E		N	A	T	U	R	A	L		G	U	S
T	E	E	N		R	O	O	S	T		S	U	N	K
	F	R	O	Z	E	N	D	A	I	Q	U	I	R	I
J	A	S	M	I	N	E		L	A	U	N	D	E	R
O	C	T	A	N	T	S		I	N	A	N	E	S	T
G	E	O	D	E	S			S	A	D	I	S	T	S

114

B	O	O	H	I	S	S			J	A	C	I	N	T	H
A	T	P	E	A	C	E			U	P	A	B	O	V	E
C	H	E	X	M	I	X			K	E	N	O	S	H	A
K	E	N			S	O	T	H	E	R	E		C	O	R
O	L	A	V		N	I	M	B	Y		D	O	S	S	
F	L	I	N	G		P	O	O		S	E	R	T	A	
F	O	R	E	S	T	S		X	T	I	M	E	S	Y	
		C	U	B				A	M	E					
T	H	E	K	I	S	S		F	T	B	R	A	G	G	
R	I	V	E	T		P	C	U		A	I	S	L	E	
I	D	I	D		S	L	A	N	T		T	A	U	T	
M	A	L		S	P	I	F	F	U	P		J	E	B	
S	W	O	O	P	I	N			A	L	A	M	O	D	E
P	A	N	C	A	K	E			C	L	I	C	K	O	N
A	Y	E	A	Y	E	S			T	E	N	C	E	N	T

115

E	S	T	E	S	■	■	■	M	S	D	O	S
M	E	A	G	E	R	■	■	P	O	M	E	L	O
B	R	O	O	D	E	R	■	C	A	L	I	B	E	R
A	G	I	T	A	T	O	■	O	V	E	R	E	A	T
Y	E	S	I	T	I	S	■	M	A	S	K	E	R	S
■	I	T	S	E	L	E	M	E	N	T	A	R	Y	■
■	S	T	R	E	S	S	T	E	S	T	S	■
■	■	■	A	T	O	■
■	L	I	T	E	R	A	T	U	R	E	S
■	F	U	T	U	R	E	R	E	S	U	L	T	S
T	I	N	S	T	A	R	■	R	U	N	L	A	P	S
R	E	C	H	O	S	E	■	M	A	N	A	T	E	E
U	S	H	E	R	E	D	■	S	L	I	M	I	N	G
S	T	E	R	E	S	■	■	S	E	A	N	C	E
T	A	S	E	D	■	■	■	R	E	G	E	R

116

S	T	R	A	I	N	E	D	P	E	A	C	H	E	S
R	O	U	N	D	A	B	O	U	T	R	O	U	T	E
I	T	S	N	O	C	O	M	P	A	R	I	S	O	N
S	O	S	■	I	H	N	■	■	I	S	L	■
■	U	N	O	■	S	A	L	■	S	U	N	G
A	B	E	N	D	■	A	W	N	■	N	O	E
C	O	N	C	E	A	L	E	D	W	E	A	P	O	N
T	O	A	L	E	S	S	E	R	E	X	T	E	N	T
I	M	M	E	D	I	A	T	E	D	A	N	G	E	R
N	E	O	■	C	O	W	■	M	O	S	S	Y
G	R	R	R	■	P	E	N	■	M	T	S	■
■	E	P	I	■	V	I	A	■	H	E	W
D	I	A	M	O	N	D	J	I	M	B	R	A	D	Y
I	T	T	A	K	E	S	A	V	I	L	L	A	G	E
D	E	E	P	E	S	T	R	E	C	E	S	S	E	S

117

R	E	B	A	■	A	N	I	T	A	■	P	R	E	S
E	R	I	C	T	H	E	R	E	D	■	H	A	L	L
D	I	N	A	H	S	H	O	R	E	■	I	I	I	I
A	N	O	D	E	■	I	N	N	S	■	L	S	A	T
■	C	E	O	S	■	■	L	I	E	N	S
A	L	U	M	■	A	C	H	■	T	A	P	S	■
T	O	L	I	T	T	L	E	P	U	R	P	O	S	E
T	R	A	C	T	I	O	N	E	N	G	I	N	E	S
A	I	R	C	O	N	D	I	T	I	O	N	E	R	S
■	V	I	P	S	■	E	E	N	■	E	S	T	O
E	M	I	R	S	■	■	G	R	E	G	■
D	I	S	C	■	I	C	E	D	■	H	A	L	A	L
N	A	I	L	■	S	L	U	I	C	E	G	A	T	E
A	T	O	E	■	L	O	R	D	N	E	L	S	O	N
S	A	N	S	■	A	T	E	I	N	■	E	S	M	E

118

D	O	H	A	Q	A	T	A	R	■	P	H	O	T	O
O	B	A	M	A	C	A	R	E	■	A	T	R	A	P
G	O	B	A	N	A	N	A	S	■	S	E	E	M	E
R	E	A	■	D	I	L	L	■	C	T	S	C	A	N
A	P	N	E	A	■	I	S	T	H	A	T	A	L	L
C	A	E	N	■	N	E	N	E	■	R	E	Y	■	■
E	R	R	O	R	■	E	A	T	S	U	P	■	■	■
S	T	O	L	A	V	■	■	T	H	E	S	O	N	■
■	■	■	A	G	E	N	T	K	■	S	T	O	N	E
P	J	S	■	S	E	A	L	■	C	R	E	W	■	■
T	A	U	B	E	T	A	P	I	■	P	O	T	T	S
B	R	I	A	R	S	■	I	N	R	I	■	D	I	D
O	U	T	T	A	■	L	O	G	I	N	N	A	M	E
A	L	O	E	S	■	I	C	E	S	K	A	T	E	S
T	E	R	S	E	■	M	A	R	K	Y	M	A	R	K

119

S	C	A	R	E	C	R	O	W	S	■	C	O	S	T
T	O	L	E	D	O	O	H	I	O	■	A	N	N	A
I	W	A	N	T	M	Y	M	T	V	■	L	E	O	N
F	E	T	E	■	B	A	S	H	■	C	L	O	W	N
F	R	E	E	R	O	L	L	■	■	R	I	C	C	I
■	■	■	I	M	E	A	N	■	A	N	T	O	N	■
■	T	H	I	N	E	■	W	O	L	F	G	A	N	G
■	H	A	N	G	A	R	■	M	O	T	I	V	E	■
W	R	I	S	T	L	E	T	■	V	I	N	E	S	■
A	E	R	E	O	■	M	A	G	E	E	■	■	■	■
R	E	S	T	S	■	C	H	A	R	T	R	E	S	■
W	H	A	M	S	■	B	O	O	P	■	W	E	L	T
I	O	L	A	■	P	O	P	U	P	V	I	D	E	O
C	L	O	P	■	C	H	I	L	L	A	X	I	N	G
K	E	N	S	■	P	R	E	S	E	N	T	D	A	Y

120

O	R	G	A	N	S	■	S	O	C	I	A	L	I	Q
N	A	U	S	E	A	■	E	D	I	T	M	E	N	U
R	U	N	S	O	N	■	T	E	R	I	Y	A	K	I
A	C	C	E	N	T	■	R	O	C	S	■	D	M	Z
M	O	A	T	■	A	M	A	N	A	■	M	O	A	N
P	U	S	S	Y	C	A	T	S	■	Z	O	R	R	O
S	S	E	■	E	R	I	E	■	K	O	P	E	K	S
■	■	E	L	U	L	■	C	A	N	E	■	■	■	■
S	C	H	U	L	Z	■	M	O	N	K	■	L	S	D
C	H	A	R	S	■	B	A	B	Y	S	P	I	C	E
H	A	L	O	■	L	E	T	B	E	■	O	T	I	C
I	T	T	■	J	E	D	I	■	W	A	S	H	E	R
S	E	E	P	E	D	I	N	■	E	L	A	I	N	E
M	A	R	I	T	I	M	E	■	S	E	D	U	C	E
S	U	S	P	E	N	S	E	■	T	E	A	M	E	D

The New York Times

SMART PUZZLES

Presented with Style

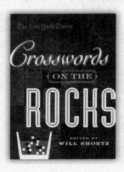

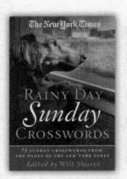